A D V O C A C Y

Court Trials ♦ Arbitrations ♦ Administrative Cases ♦ Jury Trials

EVIDENCE, OBJECTIONS, AND EXHIBITS

By

ROGER HAYDOCK

and

JOHN SONSTENG

West Publishing

West's Commitment to the Environment

In 1906, West Publishing Company began recycling materials left over from the production of books. This began a tradition of efficient and responsible use of resources. Today, more than 100% of our legal books, and 75% of our college texts are printed on acid-free, recycled paper consisting of 50% new paper pulp and 50% paper that has undergone a de-inking process. We also use soy-based inks to print many of our books. West recycles nearly 22,650,000 pounds of scrap paper annually—the equivalent of 187,500 tree. Since the 1960s, West has devised ways to capture and recycle waste inks, solvents, oils, and vapors created in the printing process. We also recycle plastics of all kinds, wood, glass, corrugated cardboard, and batteries, and have eliminated the use of styrofoam book packaging. We at West are proud of the longevity and the scope of our commitment to the environment.

West pocket parts are printed on recyclable paper and can be collected and recycled with newspapers. Staples do not have to be removed because recycling companies use magnets to extract staples during the recycling process.

The cover art, reproduced with the permission of the artist, Hank Virgona, is drawn from a series entitled, *This Honorable Profession*.

Regarding his work, the artist notes:

> "The rule of law is one of the most important pillars of freedom. As an artist who frequently uses satire to make a point, I have always kept in mind the words of Thomas Jefferson: 'the price of freedom is eternal vigilance.'
>
> "My personal observation of the courts has shown that they are only as perfect as those who run them.
>
> "In graphically depicting these observations I have tried, without judgment to show this, for only through honest appraisal can we maintain the vigilance required to safeguard this most vital element of freedom."

Hank Virgona lives and works in New York City.

To: Julie

To: Michael, David, and Molly

*

ACKNOWLEDGMENTS

Many persons contributed to the making of this book. We received substantial support and assistance from our families, friends, and colleagues. We thank them all and greatly appreciate their being a part of our lives.

The students, staff, and faculty at the William Mitchell College of Law deserve special acknowledgment. Renee Anderson, Cheri Fenstermaker, and Cal Bonde greatly assisted in developing this book. Professors Peter Knapp and Ann Juergens provided us with ideas and encouragement. David Herr and other trial lawyers also provided us with suggestions and support. Aaron Dean, Renee Fast, Tiffaney George, Anne Smith, Steve Smith, and Alexandra Schaffer provided research assistance and help.

We also acknowledge those individuals in our earlier book, *Trial: Theories, Tactics, and Techniques*. The Riley v. Garfield House Apartment trial that appears in Book 5 is based on the fact pattern developed by the Association of Trial Lawyers of America. Our publisher and editors at West also deserve our deep appreciation and thanks.

We further acknowledge you who will be reading and using this book. We have written this text for you, for the clients you represent, and the system you serve.

*

PREFACE

ADVOCACY by HAYDOCK and SONSTENG consists of five books:

> **Book 1**—Planning to Win: Effective Preparation.
>
> **Book 2**—Opening and Closing: How to Present a Case
>
> **Book 3**—Examining Witnesses: Direct, Cross, and Expert Examinations
>
> **Book 4**—Evidence, Objections, and Exhibits
>
> **Book 5**—Jury Trials

These books provide the spectrum of knowledge and skills you need to advocate a case. Each book explains the practice, rules, strategies, tactics, techniques, and theories of preparing and presenting a case. You will learn what to do, where to do it, and why to do it.

These five books explain how to be an effective advocate in all dispute resolution forums including courts, arbitrations, and administrative hearings. The materials present efficient and economical approaches to case preparation and effective approaches to trying cases before judges, jurors, arbitrators, and administrative judges. References in the text to "judges" includes judicial and administrative judges.

This series of books covers civil and criminal trials in the federal and state judicial systems, administrative proceedings, and arbitration hearings. Advocacy by Haydock and Sonsteng is the first publication of its kind to cover comprehensive advocacy skills in all these forums.

What occurs during trials, administrative cases, and arbitrations follow some common and some different rules of procedures. These materials explain both similar and differing practices. Every chapter describes alternative tactics and approaches. There is no single way to plan or present a case. Much of what occurs is determined by the advocate's approach and judgment, and examples illustrated in the text will assist you in making well-reasoned decisions.

The decisions that must be made—from the planning of what to do to the presentation of the case—are based on analytical legal reasoning and incisive judgments. Understanding how to do something and why something is done are keys to a successful case. This integrating process is a primary focus of this series of books.

Advocates make mistakes in every case, and problems commonly occur during cases. The key is not to let the mistakes and problems overwhelm or negate the presentation. Many problems can be anticipated and many mistakes can be eliminated through preparation in an understanding of available solutions described in these materials.

Ethical issues arise during the preparation and presentation of a case. An underlying premise of Advocacy by Haydock and Sonsteng is that lawyers must hold themselves to high ethical standards. An understanding of professional rules and guidelines assist in identifying ethical concerns and resolving problems.

Book One explains how to effectively, efficiently, and economically prepare and plan a case. You will learn how to be a persuasive advocate and how to tell a compelling story. You will learn how to select a case theory and develop a strategy. You will also learn how to choose a forum, select a decision maker, manage a case, anticipate problems, present evidence, identify motions, and act as an advocate. Decisions you may need to make after a case regarding post-trial and post-hearing motions and appeals are explained in case you do win and the other party cannot accept losing.

Book Two describes everything you need to know about conducting highly effective opening presentations and closing summations. Descriptions and examples of organization, structure, storytelling, persuasive approaches, improper approaches, and methods of delivery are provided. Effective ways to prepare and present a motion are also described. Did you think we were going to suggest ineffective ways?

Book Three explains all you need to effectively conduct direct and cross-examination of witnesses, including expert witnesses. The chapter on direct-examination contains strategic explanations and numerous examples of tactics and techniques that will enable you to conduct a persuasive direct examination. The chapter on cross-examination provides a complete explanation of the various types of cross-examination questions and contains numerous illustrations of successful examination approaches, including impeachment. The chapter on expert examinations provides a thorough explanation of alternative topics and questions to ask expert witnesses on direct and cross-examination. Reading this chapter will be more fun than watching Jeopardy.

Book Four comprehensively summarizes and analyzes evidentiary objections and exhibits. Specific procedures applicable to objections are explained in detail, including how to assert and pursue objections and rulings. Explanations and examples of common objections made to direct-examination and cross-examination situations are also presented. A summary compilation of the substantive rules of evidence applicable to court, arbitration, and administrative proceedings is included, including an understandable explanation of hearsay. A comprehensive chapter on exhibits provides specific explanations and examples of foundation questions necessary to introduce a variety of exhibits including common exhibits and modern demonstrative evidence. This chapter also explains the most persuasive ways to use exhibits, in an advocacy setting and at home.

Book Five explains jury selection and jury instructions. You will learn alternative theories of jury selection, how to question prospective jurors, and how to select or challenge potential jurors. You will also learn how to plan and submit jury instructions and all the rules and proceedings governing jury trials. A complete transcript of a jury trial case is included to provide you with an example of an entire jury trial from jury selection to verdict. This transcript permits you to analyze the advocacy theories, tactics, and techniques used by the attorneys, and to second and third guess them.

These books explain the whys and why nots, and the shoulds and should nots of advocacy. The chapters present numerous examples and illustrations of lawyers making presentations and examining witnesses. The examples are based on real and fictional events from the world of history, literature, art, and comedy. We selected events, parties, and witnesses that relate to the topic or skills being explained. Hopefully these illustrations will make interesting, memorable, and entertaining reading.

Our occasional attempts at humor that appear throughout the text may, with the right timing, even be funny. We often take ourselves in practice too seriously, and an occasion guffaw, moan, or snicker may help put things in proper perspective.

We hope that you are experiencing the reality of advocacy practice and its moments of adventure, frustration, excitement, challenge, and enjoyment. We encourage you to send us comments, suggestions, stories, anecdotes, and examples that we can include in our next edition. We wish you the best in being an advocate.

John Sonsteng
Roger Haydock
William Mitchell College of Law
875 Summit Avenue
St. Paul, MN 55105

February 1994

TRIAL PRACTICE TOOLS FROM WEST

Advocacy: Five Books on
Essential Skills . . . . Haydock and Sonsteng

The Common Sense Rules
of Trial Advocacy . . . . . . Evans

Bennett's Guide to Jury
Selection and Trial
Dynamics . . . . Bennett and Hirschhorn

Federal Civil Rules   Baicker-McKee, Janssen,
Handbook . . . . Berger and Corr

Federal Practice and   Wright, Miller, Kane, Cooper,
Procedure . . . . Marcus, Graham and Gold

The Trialbook: A Total System
for the Preparation and
Presentation of a Case . . . Sonsteng, Haydock and Boyd

Federal Civil Trialbook . . . . . Matthews

A Lawyer's Guide to
Effective Negotiation
and Mediation . . . . Lisnek

Depositions: Procedure,
Strategy and Technique . . Lisnek and Kaufman

Handbook of Federal
Evidence . . . . Graham

Trial Advocacy . . . . Jeans

Effective Client
Communication: A Lawyer's
Handbook for Interviewing
and Counseling . . . . . . Lisnek

Photographic Evidence . . . . Scott

Federal Jury Practice
and Instructions
Civil and Criminal . . . . . . Devitt, Blackmar, Wolff and O'Malley

Federal Court of Appeals
Manual . . . . Knibb

Federal Civil Judicial Procedure and Rules

Manual for Complex Litigation

Federal Rules of Evidence for United States Courts and Magistrates

WESTLAW®

Specialized Litigation Databases

AFJ ----------- Almanac of the Federal Judiciary
AMJTA -------- American Journal of Trial Advocacy
BNA–PLD ------ BNA Products Liability Daily
CA–JI ---------- California Jury Instructions
EXPNET -------- ExpertNet®
FSD ----------- Forensic Services Directory
LITIG ---------- Litigation
LRP–JV --------- Jury Verdicts and Settlement Summaries
LTG–TP -------- Litigation—Law Reviews, Texts and Bar Journals
MEDMAL ------- Medical Malpractice Lawsuit Filings
REST–TORT ----- Restatement of the Law—Torts
REVLITIG ------- The Review of Litigation
SCT–PREVIEW --- Preview of U.S. Supreme Court Cases
TASA ---------- Technical Advisory Service for Attorneys
WTH–MDML ---- WESTLAW Topical Highlights—Medical Malpractice
WTH–PL ------- WESTLAW Topical Highlights—Products Liability

Westfax®   **West CD–ROM Libraries™**   **Disk Products**

WESTLAW

The Ultimate Research System.

To order any of these trial practice tools, call your West
Representative or 1–800–328–9352.

NEED A NEW CASE RIGHT NOW?

You can get copies of new court cases faxed to you today—office,
courthouse or hotel, anywhere a fax machine is available. Call
WEST*fax* at 1–800–562–2329.

June 1994

BOOK FOUR
EVIDENCE,
OBJECTIONS,
AND EXHIBITS

TABLE OF CONTENTS

BOOK FOUR
EVIDENCE, OBJECTIONS, AND EXHIBITS

ANALYSIS OF SECTIONS

CHAPTER 1. OBJECTION PROCEDURES

CHAPTER 2. EVIDENTIARY OBJECTIONS

CHAPTER 3. HEARSAY

CHAPTER 4.   EXHIBITS

INTRODUCTION

This book explains evidentiary objections and the introduction and use of exhibits. Chapter One explains objection procedures and how to assert objections. Chapter Two describes evidentiary objections including the various types of common objections. Chapter Three further describes hearsay and explains available hearsay exceptions. Chapter Four explains all you need to know to introduce and use exhibits and includes numerous examples of exhibit foundations. These skills permit you to present or defend a case as well as it can be presented or defended.

*

CHAPTER 1
OBJECTION
PROCEDURES

*The opposition is indispensable . . . . A sensible human
being . . . always learns more from . . . opponents
than from . . . fervent supporters.*

— Walter Lippmann
The Independensable Opposition
Atlantic Monthly, August 1939

A. SCOPE

1.01 Why Object?

Evidentiary objections are used to exclude evidence that
should not be considered by the fact finder, or to change
the form of questions improperly phrased by opposing counsel.
Objections also may be used to control the behavior and
statements of an opposing attorney, a witness, the judge, arbitrator, hearing officer, or other participants, or to prevent a
witness from being harassed. All objections create a record of
the error and preserve that error as a ground for a new trial,
hearing or an appeal. The failure to make an objection usually
waives any error unless the error is so prejudicial and obvious
that the substantial rights of a party are adversely affected.

Objections may also accomplish tactical objectives. Tactical
reasons for objecting are only proper if there is a good faith

legal basis that supports the objection. Objections with no legal basis made solely to interrupt or bother the opposing lawyer are improper.

An attorney may tactically object to emphasize an opponent's evidentiary problems, to force the opponent to alter the introduction of evidence, or to alter the presentation of the case. An attorney may also object to help a witness testify. For example, if a witness becomes confused or has difficulty answering questions, an objection may allow the witness a short break to regain composure and plan a responsive answer. An objection may also be used to interrupt the flow of testimony. When an examination is proceeding very smoothly, an objection may break up the rhythm and flow of the examination. An experienced lawyer may object in an effort to confuse or distract an inexperienced lawyer who may become nervous and ineffectual. These tactical objectives, however, must always be supported by a good faith legal basis.

1.02 The Type of Case

Rules of evidence govern the admissibility of evidence in trials. This chapter explains evidentiary rules and tactics applicable in both bench and jury trials. While arbitrations and administrative hearings may be governed by rules of evidence, they are often leniently observed. The advocate must know how the rules are to be applied in these hearings and must discover in advance of these hearings the degree of flexibility which will govern the hearing.

Proper foundations, reliable testimony, and appropriate question format will make the evidence more persuasive. When used properly, the rules of evidence are excellent guides to persuasive advocacy. When used positively to prepare a case, to present facts and exhibits, the rules of evidence are very helpful. The concepts and practices discussed in this chapter apply to arbitrations and administrative hearings as well as trials. All of the references to judge include arbitrators and administrative hearing officers.

1.03 Evidentiary Considerations

Objections should be planned around the following considerations:

The approach.

The judge's knowledge of the rules of evidence and inclination to make rulings is a major factor. Some judges sustain minor, technically correct objections while other judges apply a broader approach and overrule such objections. The attorney who interposes too many questionable objections may lose favor with the judge. There may be little advantage in making an objection the judge will overrule. While the mere fact that the judge disagrees with the legitimacy of an objection is not a reason by itself not to object, it is a consideration.

The effect of an objection.

An objection may alert an opposing lawyer to additional areas of inquiry or indicate that certain evidence needs to be developed further. An objection may call a mistake or an omission to the attention of the opponent who may then correct the error. Objections should not be made in situations such as these where they may help the opponent.

The reaction of the fact finder.

Incessant objections, whether sustained or overruled, may alienate the fact finder. Each objection represents an interruption and a delay in the trial. Fact finders may become annoyed at a lawyer who causes the hearing to bog down. They may perceive that the objecting attorney is attempting to hide evidence or is acting unfairly.

The nature of the evidence.

A lawyer should consider objecting to anything that lacks probative value, is unclear or confusing, is collateral to the issues in dispute, or breaches an applicable rule of evidence.

Highlighting specific evidence.

An objection tends to highlight the evidence to which it is directed. For several seconds or minutes the attention of the lawyers and fact finder is focused on the evidence to which an objection has been made. A lawyer might refrain from objecting, knowing that an objection will highlight that evidence, and perhaps unduly emphasize and increase its weight.

Creation of a clear and complete record.

If something objectionable and prejudicial occurs, an objection should be made for the record to hold the offending participant accountable for such conduct. Arbitrations and administrative hearings may not have verbatim records and an appeal on the record may not be available.

Preservation of an error for post-trial motions and appeal.

Even if a lawyer anticipates that an objection will be overruled, the objection should be made to preserve the error properly.

The ability of an opponent.

An opponent may have little knowledge of evidence law and may not be able to properly ask questions or lay foundations. Sustained objections may disrupt the presentation of a poorly prepared attorney, while other opponents who understand evidentiary rules may not be ruffled by objections.

Strategic impact.

A lawyer might consider making appropriate objections, which are sure to be sustained early in the trial, even if the offered evidence is not particularly harmful. Such successful objections early in the hearing give the lawyer the appearance of being alert, in control, and knowledgeable.

1.04 What You Need to Know

This chapter explains objections to the introduction of evidence. Objections made during opening statement, summation, and jury selection appear in those respective chapters of Books Two and Five in this Advocacy Series.

B. PLANNING

1.05 How to Prepare

Objections are based on violations of the rules of evidence, statutes, trial practice, civil and criminal procedure, case law, common sense, and fairness. Not all judges recognize all objections. The understanding and interpretation of evidence law varies among them and varies depending on the type of hearing. An attorney must adapt to the rules as applied and assert those objections which are recognized.

1.06 Anticipating Evidentiary Problems

Anticipating evidentiary problems and planning how to handle them are elements of proper preparations. The goal of an examining attorney is to present evidence that is not objectionable. When preparing and presenting evidence, the attorney must recognize and understand potential objections that may be asserted and structure questions to avoid evidentiary weaknesses. The opposing attorney must anticipate potentially inadmissible evidence and prepare objections to that evidence. A motion may be brought before the trial begins or before a witness testifies to obtain a ruling on the admissibility of evidence before it is introduced.

1.07 What is Admissible and Why?

Two questions must be resolved regarding the introduction of evidence:

> Is the evidence admissible under the law?
>
> What is the weight or probative value of the evidence?

The judge decides the first question, and the fact finder (jury, judge, arbitrator, hearing officer) decides the second. Federal Rule of Evidence 104 and similar state rules require the court to make preliminary decisions regarding the admissibility of evidence. The judge reviews the sufficiency of the initial evidence and then decides whether to allow the introduction of further evidence. The judge determines whether the facts introduced are sufficient to support a finding a reasonable fact finder may make based on those facts. For example, judges decide whether sufficient evidence has been introduced to establish that a person is qualified to be a witness, that a privilege exists, that a duplicate document is admissible, and that a hearsay statement falls within an exception rendering it admissible. After sufficient evidence has been introduced, the fact finders then determine whether the admissible evidence is probative, credible, and persuasive. In situations when a close question exists regarding the sufficiency of the evidence, most judges are inclined to admit the evidence and let the jurors determine what it is worth.

In court trials, arbitrations, and administrative hearings the judge may not make pre-trial evidentiary rulings and may admit evidence that would not be admitted in a jury trial. In these cases the judge may feel able to disregard improper evidence or give it its appropriate worth in the decision making process.

1.08 How to Make Evidentiary Objections

The process of making evidentiary objections includes two separate decisions:

 Is there a legitimate, good faith available objection supported by the law of evidence?

 Is there a favorable strategic or tactical reason for making the objection?

It is difficult enough to make these decisions in a calm, cool, detached atmosphere, such as while reading this chapter. It is much more difficult to make a quick decision amidst the tension and commotion of a trial or hearing. An objecting attorney must make split-second judgments while concentrating on everything else happening. This skill is developed with practice and experience, and with more practice and experience. That, of course, takes time. There are a number of things that can be done by inexperienced lawyers to increase their ability to think quickly, make instant judgments, and assert objections:

BECOME FAMILIAR with the types of common objections. Review a list of available objections and organize the objections in a format that permits you to easily remember and apply these objections. An organized list and an objection planning worksheet may group objections by topic or categorize them by the evidence rules.

LEARN TO RECOGNIZE types or patterns of evidence that create objectionable situations. These include:

—Lengthy direct examination questions are often objectionable because they are leading.

—Questions that involve conversations may trigger hearsay objections.

—Questions calling for the witness' observations require proper foundation and may be objectionable based on a lack of foundation.

—Questions calling for a lay witness to give an opinion may give rise to an objection based on an improper conclusion.

—Documents must be authenticated, otherwise an objection based on lack of authentication may be appropriate.

—Answers that include prefaces such as "I'm not certain, but . . ." may support an objection based on speculation.

IN ADVANCE, PREPARE a list of specific objections to the anticipated evidence. This planning process will assist in quickly and accurately identifying objections.

CONCENTRATE on the evidence being introduced. Although many things are going on while the evidence is being introduced, concentrate on the evidence. Try to avoid reviewing cross-examination questions or vacation plans.

LISTEN ATTENTIVELY and watch the examination. The sound of a question or answer, or the demeanor of the attorney or witness, may be objectionable or may make a question or response objectionable.

RELY ON COMMON SENSE. Relying in part on an intuitive or instinctive reaction that something is wrong is an effective way to identify an objectionable situation.

OVER PREPARE. Extra preparation helps in applying the rules of evidence to the evidence introduced at trial.

BE PREPARED to lose an objection. Don't be overly concerned when the judge says "Overruled." Valid objections are often overruled and inadmissible evidence is sometimes admitted.

BE WILLING to make mistakes. Expect that the judge will disagree with your objections and think you are wrong. Sometimes you will be.

PREPARE TO BE SURPRISED. Sometimes judges exercise their discretion in very strange ways.

ANTICIPATE the unexpected. Even though you believe that you know what the evidence will be, it may come in differently, requiring an appropriate response. Be alert for the unexpected.

SEE IF THE JUDGE wants you to object. The judge may invite an objection by non-verbal signals or by appearing impatient with the testimony. An attorney should not, however, necessarily object at the judge's apparent invitation. The attorney may misinterpret the judge's behavior, or the attorney may not want to object for tactical reasons.

REHEARSE making objections to anticipated evidentiary problems. Imagine how opposing counsel may attempt to introduce inadmissible evidence and how witnesses may improperly respond. Then imagine asserting objections in these scenarios.

PRACTICE during casual conversations. When talking with family and friends, practice objecting to things they say. For example, if they start spreading gossip, object "hearsay," which will help you apply and understand hearsay rules. This practice may result in your spending more time by yourself, but it's fun for a while.

1.09 Deciding Whether to Make Objections

Whether an objection should be made—even when there is legal support for the objection and the judge will most likely sustain the objection—depends on the strategic impact the objection has on the admissibility of the evidence. The more critical the evidence is to the theories of the case, the more likely the objection should be made. There are four basic guidelines determining whether to object to inadmissible evidence:

   If the evidence is clearly admissible, the lawyer should not object. Rather, the attorney should try to minimize the effect of the evidence through cross-examination or rebuttal and then argue its lack of weight in final argument.

   If the offered evidence is clearly inadmissible and harmful, the lawyer should object. The law of evidence should be used to exclude harmful evidence.

   If the evidence is probably inadmissible but not harmful, the attorney should consider not objecting, or may object but not pursue the issue if the judge overrules the objection. The potential problem of weak evidence may be overcome on cross-examination or final argument. The lawyer may establish on cross-examination that the testimony or witness is unreliable, and can argue the slight probative value or the implausibility of the evidence during final argument.

   If the answer to a question will reveal favorable or neutral information, then no objection should be made.

In many situations, there may be no need to interpose objections. Cases tried between skilled and well prepared lawyers are often tried with few or no objections.

1.10 Making Alternative Objections

There may be more than one objection that can be made to a question or an answer. Part of the planning process is formulating a series of potential objections to anticipated evidence. Objections that may be available to the same piece of evidence, such as:

Improper form of the question.
The question may be leading or otherwise improper.

Irrelevant.
The topic may not have any logical relevance to the case.

Cumulative.
The evidence has previously been introduced and this item of evidence is unnecessarily repetitive.

Unfairly prejudicial.
Even if the item is relevant, it may be unfairly prejudicial.

Lack of foundation.
The witness may not be competent to lay a foundation for the introduction of this item of evidence.

Improper opinion.
The witness may testify to an inadmissible opinion.

Hearsay.
The source of the information the witness knows may be from an inadmissible hearsay source.

Original writing (best evidence) required.
The evidence is being offered to prove the contents of a writing, and the writing must be introduced.

Ouch! It hurts.
You are losing and the evidence hurts that much more.

1.11 Explaining Why No Objection is Made

In some situations an objection may seem appropriate, but the attorney does not want to object. In such situations, the attorney may want to explain why no objection is being made. Instead of sitting silently the attorney may state: "We want the court or jurors to hear this testimony," or "We agree that the fact finder should see this exhibit," or "We want the arbitrators to review this evidence."

1.12 Accepting an Objection Invitation

Judges occasionally look at opposing counsel when evidence is being introduced and ask "Any objection?" Some judges ask these questions neutrally without suggesting that an objection exists in order to provide opposing lawyers with an opportunity to interpose an objection. Other judges do this to signal that they will sustain an appropriate objection. An attorney should not object merely because the judge believes an objection ought to be made, but rather the attorney should reconsider and assert an objection if a strategic reason exists for doing so. A judge less frequently may look at opposing counsel and ask "Do you have a clue about what you are doing?" Be thankful it's not you.

C. HOW TO PRESENT OBJECTIONS

1.13 How to Object

Whether an attorney should stand or remain seated while objecting depends on the jurisdiction and judge. Most judges expect the attorney to stand when addressing the court. The seated attorney may say "Objection, your Honor," and then stand to state the grounds. The extra half second gained by standing may help in framing an objection. An attorney may remain seated or request to remain seated, especially if the objection is made quickly and the judge immediately rules, or if there is a series of objections. In jury trials, most objections and rulings are made in front of jurors unless an argument must be made on the objection.

1.14 When to Object

An objection must be timely made. If a question is improper, the objection must be made before the answer is given. For example, objections to the form of a question must be made immediately after the question and before the answer. If a question is proper but the response is inadmissible, an objection should be made as soon as the inadmissible evidence becomes apparent. For example, if a witness begins to testify to inadmissible hearsay, the opposing attorney should interrupt and make an objection. An objection interjected too late, however meritorious, is ordinarily overruled by the judge. Late objections are also ineffective because the fact finder has already heard part or all of the inadmissible evidence. Furthermore, the error may not be preserved for appeal.

Attorneys should avoid making premature objections. If an objection to the content of a statement is available, the attorney must object to the question that introduces the objectionable content. For example, an objection to the preliminary question, "Do you have an opinion about the defendant's condition?" is premature, but the attorney should object to the follow-up question seeking an improper opinion, "What is that opinion?" Similarly, a hearsay objection to the question, "Did you have a conversation with the witness?" is premature, the proper objection should be made to the next question, "What did the witness say?"

This task is made more difficult by the fact that witnesses often are not prepared to respond to the precise wording of the questions. The question "Do you have an opinion?" often produces the opinion rather than the anticipated "Yes" answer. If the examiner has not adequately prepared the witness, an objection may have to be made to the preliminary question in order to prevent these nonresponsive answers. The judge may, however, overrule the premature objection, and the attorney will need to restate the objection following the next question.

Sample Dialogues

Examining Attorney:

Q: Did you and Ms. Wells-Barney speak to each other?

Objecting Lawyer:

I object your Honor, that question calls for hearsay.

Judge:

The objection is premature, the witness may answer.

A: Yes, we did.

Q: What did Ms. Wells-Barney say?

Objecting Lawyer:

Objection, hearsay.

Judge:

Sustained.

When the witness responds to a question calling for a yes or no answer with a further response, the attorney should object to the answer because it goes beyond the scope of the question.

Examining Attorney:

Q: Dr. Oppenheimer, do you have an opinion as to the effectiveness of the Fermi Accelerator?

A: Yes, I do. It is probably the only . . .

Objecting Lawyer:

Your Honor, I object. The question has been answered.

Judge:

Sustained.

The witness should stop answering the question once the objection is made. If the witness continues to answer, the opposing attorney should interrupt and ask the judge to instruct the witness to stop answering. If the examining attorney is asking questions too rapidly, or if the witness is answering questions too quickly, the judge may be asked to instruct the attorney or witness to proceed at a reasonable pace, which provides an opportunity to object before the witness responds.

1.15 How to Phrase an Objection

The proper way to object in most jurisdictions is to say "objection" and state the specific ground or grounds with a few identifying words. This method is simple, quick, and advises the judge of the ground(s) of the objection. The applicable rules of evidence ordinarily require the objecting attorney to state the specific reason supporting the objection. See, e.g., Fed.R.Evid. 103(a)(1). More than one ground may support an objection, and an attorney should state all applicable grounds. However, it is inappropriate to state all evidentiary objections in alphabetical order in the desperate hope that one of them applies. If the attorney does not advance a specific reason yet the ground for the objection is apparent from the context of the evidence, an objection may still be sustained by the judge.

Using the name or title of the rule involved is usually sufficient: "Your Honor, objection, hearsay" or "We object, your Honor, on the grounds of hearsay." Also, the addition of a descriptive term to an objection in a jury trial is advisable so the jury better understands the grounds for the objection: "Objection, unreliable hearsay." Some judges expect attorneys to use specific words in making an objection, requiring the attorneys to be very precise. Other judges require objecting attorneys to refer to specific evidence rule numbers. Fortunately, these judges are phew! in number.

1.16 Talk Quietly in Front of the Jury

Jury proceedings should be conducted so that inadmissible evidence, arguments, and statements are not heard by the jury. Comments by counsel, arguments, lengthy objections, and offers of proof must be made outside the hearing of the jury. Jurors should not be influenced by inadmissible evidence or the explanations of counsel.

"Speaking objections"—arguments in front of the jury—are rarely appropriate. If an attorney needs to explain an objection further, permission to approach the bench should be requested and the arguments made at the bench. If an objecting attorney persists in arguing an objection in front of the jury, the other lawyer should interrupt and request permission to approach the bench. When an attorney argues at a bench conference, in a voice loud enough for jurors to hear, the judge should be asked to quiet the attorney and instruct the jury to disregard the argument.

A fine line exists between appropriate, descriptive statements and improper speaking objections. For example, an objection may be stated: "Counsel is attempting to present unreliable and untrustworthy hearsay through this witness." This statement explains the grounds of the objection and helps the jury understand the evidentiary problem. While some judges may allow this, others prohibit even a statement of this limited length.

An attorney needs to adapt objection procedures to the judge's preferences. Some judges prefer a lengthier explanation of an objection instead of a few descriptive words, and the attorney should provide the judge with that information. In jury trials some judges inappropriately allow "speaking objections" instead of requiring bench conferences. This practice results in attorneys making evidentiary arguments in front of the jury.

1.17 The Applicable Law

When an anticipated objection is made to a vital piece of evidence, it is sometimes useful to have a short, one or two page memorandum supporting or opposing the objection. This issue brief provides the judge with precedent, eliminates the need to make an extemporaneous argument, and shows the judge that the attorney is serious about a position. These factors may sway the judge regarding a close evidentiary ruling.

1.18 Your Demeanor

Objections should be made in a firm, clear voice and in a professional and reasonable manner. Objections and responses should always be directed to the judge and not to opposing counsel. Arguing with opposing counsel may draw an admonition from the judge and should be avoided. Responses to adverse rulings by the judge should also be professional and respectful. Statements of disapproval or nonverbal behavior demonstrating disappointment are usually inappropriate and rarely necessary even to highlight outrageous improper evidence or conduct.

1.19 Responding to the Judge

An attorney may need to respond to a judge who attempts to unduly restrict the attorney's ability to make or explain objections on the record. Judges want the case to proceed as quickly as possible, and some judges pressure attorneys not to make objections. Occasionally a judge may make comments in front of the jurors about what the judge perceives to be wasteful and time consuming objections. The attorney cannot always please the judge or do whatever the judge demands. It is the responsibility of the attorney, not the judge, to prevent the opposing attorney from introducing inadmissible evidence and to preserve a record for appeal. If the judge improperly interferes with the assertion of objections, the objecting attorney may make a record that the judge's interference is adversely affecting the case.

1.20 Making Continuing Objections

If an objection has been overruled and subsequent questions are asked on the same subject, the objecting attorney may consider making a "continuing" objection to every subsequent question and answer on the subject. A continuing objection may eliminate the need for the attorney to object repeatedly after each question or answer. Not all jurisdictions recognize continuing objections. A problem with their use is that there is no specific objection on the record to individual questions or answers, and it may be unclear regarding what questions and answers are included in the objection.

The lawyer should define the scope of the continuing objection as precisely as possible. Instead of saying, "I object to this entire line of questioning," the attorney should say, "I object to all the testimony about the witness' identification of Plaintiff's Exhibit No. 8 on the ground that . . . ." The lawyer should also be alert to additional grounds that arise during subsequent testimony. If another ground becomes apparent during the line of questioning, that ground should be added to the continuing objection. If the scope or grounds cannot be made clear with a continuing objection, a more effective tactic may be to repeat objections to specific questions and answers. While repetitive objections may be annoying and disruptive, they do remove any doubt regarding the ground and scope of the objection and avoid the inadvertent waiver of objections.

1.21 Responding to Objections

Usually the examining attorney need not say anything in response to an objection. Sometimes the judge asks the examining attorney to argue against the objection. In jury trials, the examining attorney wants to make a brief statement in opposition to an objection, it may be stated in front of the jury.

If the attorney wants to argue further, the attorney should approach the bench and make the argument there.

1.22 Presenting Contrary Evidence

An objecting attorney may have an opportunity to introduce contrary evidence before a judge rules on an objection which seeks to exclude evidence. Contrary evidence is evidence which establishes that an objection should be sustained. These situations arise when a judge must determine whether sufficient evidence exists to support the admissibility of additional evidence, or if there is a factual or legal impediment to further testimony.

There are two ways an opposing attorney may introduce contrary evidence. The first and typical way is by questioning the witness to lay the grounds for an objection. The second way, which is used only in unusual circumstances, is through extrinsic evidence.

1.23 Questioning the Witness

The most common way for an attorney to introduce contrary evidence is to request permission to interrupt the examination to ask questions of the witness for the purpose of establishing the grounds for an objection. The procedure—also known as "voir dire" of a witness—consists of the attorney examining the witness, usually through leading questions, to establish facts in support of ruling by the judge that subsequent evidence is inadmissible. For example, the witness may be asked to identify a document or describe an object. The opposing attorney may question the witness in an attempt to show the witness cannot sufficiently authenticate the document or has no basis for describing an object.

Judges permit "voir dire" questioning of a witness if the attorney appears able to establish the inadmissibility of the evidence. Usually the opposing attorney can ask a reasonable number of questions to establish the lack of admissibility. These questions, which interrupt the direct examination, may not develop into questions that should be asked on cross-examination. Questions that go to the weight or importance of particular evidence and which are not directed towards admissibility are improper. Questioning that extends beyond proper "voir dire" and into cross-examination should be objected to as improper and beyond the scope of appropriate voir dire. Some lawyers attempt to use "voir dire" to disrupt the direct examination. This tactic is improper unless there is a good faith basis to establish contrary evidence supporting the objection.

Sample Dialogue

Q: Ms. Chiles, please describe all the contents of the frozen
       pizza that you purchased.

Objecting Lawyer:
       Your Honor, may I voir dire the witness by asking a
       few questions to lay the foundation for an objection?

Judge:
       Yes, you may.

Objecting Lawyer:
Q: You are not a food scientist are you?
A: No.
Q: You did not test any of the ingredients in the pizza did
       you?
A: No.
Q: You did not read the label did you?
A: No.
Q: You never ate the pizza?
A: No.
Q: And by looking at it you could not tell precisely what it
       was made of.
A: That's for sure.

To the Court:

> Your Honor, I object to any further testimony by this witness about the contents of the pizza on the grounds of lack of foundation.

Judge:

> Sustained.

1.24 Presenting Extrinsic Evidence

Extrinsic evidence is evidence from a source other than the witness on the stand, such as another witness or document. Extrinsic evidence may be admissible if an opposing attorney challenges the competency of a witness or claims the existence of a privilege. For example, a witness testifies on direct examination that she is not married to the defendant and that she had a conversation with the defendant. The opposing attorney may object on the grounds of marital privilege and offer into evidence a marriage certificate as extrinsic evidence. The primary reason the situations involving the use of extrinsic evidence are rare is that these problems are usually taken care of through a motion in limine before trial or before the witness testifies.

D. EVIDENTIARY RULINGS

1.25 Ah, Discretion

Judges have broad discretion in ruling on the admissibility of evidence. The standards are more strictly applied in jury trials. The application of standards in court trials, arbitrations and administrative hearings are more varied and are often more liberal and flexible. Judges in all matters will enforce reasonable objections and in every case well presented evidence supported by appropriate foundations will be more persuasive. The standard judges use to determine the admissibility of evidence is whether there exists "evidence sufficient to support a finding" of the proposition sought to be proven. See Fed.R.Evid. 104(a) and (b). If there is insufficient evidence to support a finding regarding that proposition, the evidence is inadmissible.

1.26 Oh, the Ruling

Ordinarily, the judge rules immediately after an objection and says "sustained" (the objection is valid) or "overruled" (the objection is denied). Usually the judge does not state a reason for the ruling because the reason is the same ground the objecting attorney stated. Many judges do not sustain an objection unless the opposing lawyer correctly states the ground for the objection. While judges have the discretion to exclude inadmissible evidence on their own (in the absence of any objection or in the absence of any specific supporting grounds), many do not exercise this discretion.

1.27 Is it a Provisional Ruling?

In some situations, a judge may make a provisional, or conditional, ruling which the judge can reconsider at a later time. The judge reserves the opportunity to change the ruling depending on subsequent events that may affect the admissibility of the evidence. Objections based on irrelevancy, lack of foundation, or improper lay or expert opinion may result in conditional rulings that allow evidence to be admitted subject to reconsideration. For example, a judge may overrule a relevancy objection because the examining lawyer advises the judge that the relevancy of this evidence (Evidence A) depends upon the later admission of related evidence (Evidence B). The judge may overrule the objection and allow Evidence A on the condition that Evidence B is later presented. If Evidence B is not subsequently admitted, the objecting attorney may renew the objection to Evidence A and the judge will sustain the objection.

Sample Dialogue

Examining Attorney:

> Your Honor, at this time we offer Plaintiff's Exhibit No. 35. We realize that we need to provide another witness in order to establish the technical foundation for chain of custody. We will do that through Ms. Phaedra, who is not available as a witness until tomorrow. We are asking the court to provisionally admit Exhibit No. 35 with our assurances that we will connect up the foundation with Ms. Phaedra.

Judge:

> With that assurance I will conditionally accept Plaintiff's Exhibit No. 35 into evidence.

1.28　Inquiring About a Ruling

If an objection is sustained and the judge's reasoning is unclear, the examining attorney may ask the judge to explain the ruling. In some jurisdictions, the attorney even has a right to such an explanation. The judge may ask the objecting lawyer to explain the ground for the objection.

If the examining lawyer believes the judge made an incorrect ruling, the attorney may request that the judge reconsider the ruling. Judges do not often change their rulings, and this tactic may waste time. The judge may simply have an understanding of evidence—whether right or wrong—that is different from the lawyer's, and no purpose is served by arguing with the judge. If, for example, the judge sustained a leading objection, the examining lawyer should merely rephrase the question rather than trying to persuade the judge that the situation created an exception to the leading question rule. However, in some situations an explanation to the judge of the reasons that support the question or answer may be effective. For example, the judge may sustain a relevancy objection because the judge does not see any issue that the evidence supports. An explanation of the issue and its connection with the facts may cause the judge to change the ruling and allow the evidence.

1.29　Renewing an Objection

If the judge overrules an objection, the opposing lawyer can ask permission to make an argument in support of the objection. Judges often refuse this request because they are confident of their decision. A more effective practice for the opposing lawyer is to object to the next related question or answer. Perhaps the judge will understand the grounds for the objection better as it applies to the subsequent question or answer and sustain it.

1.30　Pursuing Objections

A judge may overrule an objection that is premature. The attorney should make objections to subsequent questions to make certain the judge rules consistently. For example, an attorney may make a "no foundation" objection to the question "Did you form an opinion after your examination?" anticipating that the witness may blurt out the opinion and give a narrative response instead of a "yes" or "no" answer. The judge may overrule the objection because this yes or no answer is permissible. The attorney then should interpose objections to subsequent questions regarding the content of the opinion.

1.31　Obtaining a Ruling

A judge may fail to make a ruling on an objection, either by mistake or as an attempt to avoid deciding. Some judges have figured out that if they don't make any ruling they can't be reversed on appeal for making a wrong ruling. It is not always easy to get a reluctant judge to rule, nevertheless attorneys have a right to a ruling and should insist on one.

Sample Dialogue

Examining Attorney:

  Q: What did Mr. Morse say about this new invention?

Objecting Lawyer:

      Objection, hearsay.

Judge:

      All right, go on, continue.

Objecting Lawyer:

      Your Honor, before we continue, I objected to the last question on the grounds of hearsay.

Judge:

      Overruled.

Witness:

  A: He said, "What hath God wrought?"

Examining Attorney:

  Q: Whom was he quoting?

Objecting Lawyer:

      Objection, irrelevant.

Judge:

      Next question.

Examining Attorney:

      Your Honor, may the witness answer the last question?

Judge:

      No, sustained.

Examining Attorney:

      Your Honor, may we approach the bench to make an offer of proof?

Judge:

      You may.

E. MOTION IN LIMINE

1.32 What Is It?

A motion in limine (meaning at the threshold) seeks an advance ruling from the judge regarding the admissibility or inadmissibility of evidence. In criminal cases, these rulings are commonly sought through suppression motions to attack the admissibility of evidence on the grounds that the evidence violates constitutional rights, statutory provisions, or the rules of evidence. See, e.g., Fed.R.Crim.P. 41. Motions in limine are also common in civil cases to obtain an advance evidentiary ruling.

1.33 Why Would You?

Motions in limine may be brought for several purposes:

> TO PROHIBIT opposing counsel from introducing or mentioning objectionable evidence. A ruling can be sought prohibiting the use of evidence that is barred by any exclusionary rule of evidence, such as unfairly prejudicial and irrelevant evidence and inadmissible hearsay. A favorable ruling prevents the fact finders from becoming aware of, and being influenced by, inadmissible evidence and from suspecting that the objecting attorney is trying to hide evidence from them. Examples of this type of evidence include the questionable admissibility of a prior criminal conviction of a party, or of subsequent remedial measures taken by a defendant in a tort case.

> TO REQUIRE opposing counsel to obtain a ruling on admissibility before evidence is offered. This motion in limine seeks a ruling from the judge requiring opposing counsel to lay a proper and complete foundation before the evidence will be admitted. Examples of such evidence include the foundation required to authenticate a document and the foundation required to comply with the original writing (best evidence) rule.

> TO OBTAIN a preliminary ruling by the court that evidence offered by the proponent is admissible. This motion is

made by the proponent of the evidence who seeks an advance ruling by the court that certain evidence will be admitted. A proponent may have some evidence which the opposing party will oppose. The proponent of this evidence may want to know prior to trial whether the evidence will be admitted in order to properly prepare and plan. Examples of this type of evidence include photographs that contain relevant but grisly depictions, or expensive demonstrative evidence. Before parties spend money creating an elaborate chart, a complicated model, or a videotape, they may prefer to obtain a preliminary ruling that such demonstrative evidence can be used. A motion in limine brought for this purpose presupposes that the opposing party plans to object to its introduction. The advantage of this type of motion is the certainty obtained by a ruling assuring an attorney that certain evidence can be referred to during opening statement. The disadvantages are that the importance of certain evidence is highlighted and opposing lawyers may be prompted to object where otherwise they may not have done so.

Motions in limine are commonly brought prior to jury trials to avoid the prejudicial impact of inadmissible evidence on the jurors, but they also serve a purpose in other hearings and trials. Obtaining an advance ruling makes clear what questionable evidence is or is not admissible. This ruling will assist in determining what the most effective theory of the case will be and what facts will be considered by the judge.

1.34 Motion in Limine Procedure

Motions in limine may be made either in writing or orally, depending on the nature of the issue and local rules. There is usually no specific limit regarding the number of motions that may be brought, but strategy and common sense ordinarily restrict such motions to important items of evidence. A judge who faces a barrage of motions regarding routine evidentiary problems may be inclined not to consider such motions seriously.

Motions in limine usually require that reasonable, advance notice be given to the opposing attorney. The timing of the notice depends on the nature of the motion, the rules of the jurisdiction, and the evidence in question. Many jurisdictions require that motions in limine be brought in writing a reasonable time prior to trial to provide the opponent with an opportunity to respond. Other courts permit motions in limine to be made orally on the eve of trial and during trial. If a party plans to offer or seeks to exclude questionable or critical evidence, it is best to submit a written motion with notice to the opposing attorney so that memoranda can be submitted and a full hearing held on the issues. When an attorney seeks to introduce or oppose the introduction of routine real evidence or standard demonstrative evidence, an oral request made before the matter is to be heard or just before a witness testifies may be sufficient.

A motion in limine should state the specific relief sought and the grounds supporting the motion. Supporting authorities should be provided to the judge in a written memo form or by providing the court with copies of supportive rules, decisions or statutes. The moving attorney should also make clear during argument why an evidentiary motion is brought in advance rather than as an ordinary objection during the hearing. Many judges prefer deferring or denying motions in limine until they see and hear the evidence that is introduced. A moving attorney has to overcome this predisposition by explaining why a preliminary ruling is necessary.

1.35 Limine Order

Any order granting the in limine motion must specify the evidence that is excluded or ruled inadmissible. An order that is overly broad may exclude otherwise admissible evidence and become the ground for a new trial or reversible error. An order that is ambiguous may permit opposing counsel to refer to related evidence while still complying with the order. If there is any doubt about the scope or meaning of an order, counsel should ask to have the order clarified.

A judge has broad discretion and several options when ruling on a motion in limine:

The judge **may refuse** to hear the motion because it is untimely. Advance written notice of a motion provided to the opposing attorney and to the judge prevents the opposing attorney from claiming surprise and prejudice and reduces the likelihood the judge will refuse to hear the motion.

The judge **may defer** ruling on the motion until later. The judge may reconsider the motion immediately prior to the time evidence is sought to be introduced. The judge may decide it is impossible or difficult to make an advance ruling because it is not clear from the arguments whether the evidence is admissible or inadmissible. The judge may prefer to wait until the evidence is developed and observe how the evidence is being introduced before making a ruling.

The judge **may deny** the motion but permit the moving attorney to bring the motion again during the hearing for the judge's reconsideration. A judge may do this for the same reasons that were explained in the previous paragraph.

The judge **may grant** only part of the relief sought in the motion in limine. If the motion seeks to totally exclude a piece of evidence, the judge may permit a part of the evidence to be introduced. Or, if the motion seeks to exclude evidence which is offered to prove several things, the judge may limit the effect of the evidence to prove only some of those things.

The judge **may enter** a conditional order requiring that specific facts be introduced as a condition for the intro-duction of the disputed evidence. If the specific facts are not introduced, the conditional ruling takes effect and the evidence is precluded. A conditional order is sometimes entered when the judge needs to hear certain facts in order to make a proper evidentiary ruling.

The judge **may grant** the motion in limine and preclude any introduction and reference, direct or indirect, to the inadmissible evidence.

The judge **may urge** the lawyers to dismiss the case and spend their time writing a law review article on the correct pronunciation of "limine."

1.36 Preserving Error

A judge's ruling on a motion in limine usually preserves that evidentiary issue as a ground for a new trial or hearing and an appeal when available. In most jurisdictions, there need not be any further evidentiary offer or objection made because the previous ruling is on the record. In some jurisdictions, a party who loses a motion in limine may need to take further steps during the hearing to preserve the evidentiary issue. In these jurisdictions, if a motion in limine is denied, the losing attorney may need to object to the introduction of the evidence during the trial to preserve the issue properly.

1.37 Violation of Order

The violation of an order granting a motion in limine may result in reversible error, especially in a jury trial if the judge does not properly instruct the jury to disregard the excluded evidence. The intentional violation of an order should also subject the offending attorney to disciplinary sanctions. Sanctions may include a reprimand and the imposition of attorney's fees. An inadvertent violation of an order may be excusable if it is not the result of negligence. Attorneys have an obligation to inform their witnesses of the effect of a ruling on a motion in limine. If the judge grants a motion and excludes evidence, the attorney must advise witnesses not to volunteer such evidence.

1.38 Example of Motion and Order

Motion in Limine

Defendant Mark Craig moves for an order in limine ordering that the Plaintiff, St. Elsewhere Hospital, makes no reference to the contract between St. Elsewhere and Mark Craig dated August 15, 1989, on the grounds that it is irrelevant and unfairly prejudicial. Defendant supports this motion with a memorandum of law and a proposed order in limine.

Order in Limine

The Defendant Mark Craig's motion in limine is granted and Plaintiff, St. Elsewhere Hospital, is ordered to make no reference to the August 15, 1989 contract between Mark Craig and St. Elsewhere Hospital.

F. OBJECTION PROCEDURES

1.39 Offers of Proof

When an objection is sustained and evidence excluded, the examining attorney must make an offer of proof to preserve the error for appellate review. The offer of proof provides a description of the excluded evidence so the appellate court can review the offered evidence and determine the significance of its exclusion. A well stated and persuasive offer of proof may also convince the judge to reconsider and change a previous ruling.

There are three ways to make an offer of proof. All these involve an explanation to the judge of the anticipated testimony and the grounds for its admissibility.

(1) Summary Offer of Proof

A summary of the evidence is the most common way of making an offer of proof:

Examining Attorney:

Q: During that afternoon conversation, what was the first
       thing Ms. Lopez said to you?

Objecting Lawyer:

       Objection, hearsay.

Judge:

       Sustained.

Examining Attorney:

       Your Honor, may I make an offer of proof?

Judge:

       Yes.

Examining Attorney:

       Judge, if you permit, the witness will testify that Ms.
       Lopez told him that she had known that the repairs
       on the golf cart were not completed on July 1.

(2) Question/Answer Offer of Proof

This method is the most time consuming but is also the most
complete and accurate. Such a format reflects the exact questions and answers that will be offered as evidence.

(3) Submission of Written Testimony as Offer

This method is used primarily in situations where the record
should contain an exact transcript of the precise evidence to be
offered.

1.40 Reconsideration of Ruling

The offer of proof provides an opportunity for the judge to
reconsider the original ruling. Sometimes, after hearing
the proposed evidence, the judge understands why it is not
objectionable and overrules the objection. The offer of proof
also provides an opportunity for the examining lawyer to explain why the evidence is admissible. This argument, coupled

with proposed evidence, may convince the judge to admit the evidence.

Example

Examining Attorney:

> Judge, at the time Ms. Lopez made the statement about the golf cart repairs she was still an employee of the defendant, and the statement is an admissible party admission.

Objecting Lawyer:

> Your Honor, Ms. Lopez did not have personal knowledge of the repairs.

Judge:

> An employee need not have personal knowledge if the statement refers to matters within the scope of employment. I will change my ruling and overrule the objection.

1.41 Motion to Strike

A motion to strike usually occurs after an attorney has made an objection and the court has granted the relief. The purpose of the motion is to make clear that the improper statement or inadmissible evidence is not to be considered by the fact finder. Although a motion to strike may clarify the scope and extent of the excluded evidence, a motion to strike is usually not necessary and should not be made unless it serves a valid purpose, or unless making such a motion is a common practice in the jurisdiction. A motion to go on strike during the case is always improper.

1.42 Request for Curative Instruction in a Jury Trial

In a jury trial a motion for a curative instruction attempts to repair the harm done by an improper question or inadmissible answer. After an objection has been sustained, the attorney may immediately ask the judge to instruct the jurors that they must disregard what they heard. It may be difficult for a juror to ignore facts and even more so when the facts have received extra attention and an instruction to disregard. However, when significant inadmissible facts have been presented, a curative instruction may be the only way to diminish harm done by these facts. The jurors may be held to their duty to disregard inadmissible testimony in the final argument and through the judge's final instructions. If told that they cannot consider some inadmissible evidence, jurors try to comply, particularly if the party causing the error appears to be acting unfairly.

Example

Objecting Lawyer:

> Objection, your Honor. The response from the witness is inadmissible hearsay and I ask that the jury be instructed to disregard that answer.

Judge:

> Members of the Jury, you are to disregard the testimony concerning the conversation between this witness and Saint Augustine.

1.43 Limited Admissibility

Evidence which is admissible for one purpose but not for another may be admitted by the court. An attorney may request that evidence be admitted for a limited purpose. See Fed.R.Evid. 105. For example, a repair bill may be admissible to prove that the bill was paid, but inadmissible hearsay to prove that actual repairs were completed. The bill can be received in evidence only for the limited purpose of proving it was paid.

A judge has several options in determining what to do with evidence that is admissible to prove some facts but not others:

The court could admit the evidence and consider if for the purpose admitted or in a jury trial instruct the jury regarding its import.

The court could admit the evidence without comment.

The court could exclude the evidence if it is unfairly prejudicial and the impact outweighs the probative value of the evidence.

The first option is probably the most common solution. The court admits the evidence but limits its scope.

Example

Judge:

> Members of the Jury, some evidence in this case is now being introduced for a limited purpose. When you receive this evidence now, and when you consider it during your deliberations, you are to use it only for (state proper purpose). You are not to use it for any other purpose. You are not to use it for (state prohibited purpose). You are only to use it (repeat proper purpose).

The judge may repeat the limiting instruction after the evidence has been received or a line of questioning completed, depending upon the nature and impact of the evidence. Further, a judge usually repeats the limiting instruction during final jury instructions at the end of the case.

Admission of evidence for a limited purpose has limitations. The fact finder who hears the evidence may disregard the limiting instructions and broadly use the evidence to prove other matters. For example, if the repair bill is received with a limiting instruction, the fact finder may nonetheless infer that the repairs were properly completed because the party would not pay the bill unless the repairs were done.

1.44 Objections to Court Questioning

All jurisdictions permit a judge to ask questions of witnesses in a bench trial, arbitration and administrative hearing. Most jurisdictions, including federal courts, provide the judge with discretion to ask questions of a witness in a jury trial. Many judges do not ask any questions of witnesses because they do not believe it is their role to do so. Judges may ask questions to clarify an important matter, and others may periodically ask questions to supplement the questions asked by the attorneys. Whatever approach the judge takes, a judge may not take over the questioning of a witness, unnecessarily interfere in witness examinations, or in a jury trial unduly influence jurors by questioning witnesses.

An attorney may object to any question asked by a judge that violates a rule of evidence. This objection is difficult to make because the attorney is challenging the judge and may be concerned about the possibility of alienating the judge who has asked the question. Further, the judge is not apt to sustain an objection to the question asked. Nonetheless, the attorney should object to exclude inadmissible evidence and to make a record for appeal. It is, of course, easier said than done, but it may need to be done.

Example

The family of a mentally handicapped patient sues the state for causing his injuries. The plaintiff is called as a witness. The judge has trouble understanding him, interrupts and asks the following questions.

Judge:

Q: You said your nurse hit you, Mr. McMurphy. Now, when did that happen?

A: When it snowed.

Q: And she hit you every time it snowed?

Objecting Lawyer:

> I object to the court's questions. Your Honor, your question was leading and may place undue weight on the response.

Most state court systems prohibit a judge from commenting on or expressing opinions about the evidence in a jury trial. State judges usually adhere to this policy and do not comment on the evidence.

The federal court system permits judges to comment on the evidence and express opinions on the weight or sufficiency of the evidence and the credibility of witnesses. Federal judges often make such comments at the time they instruct the jurors. If a federal judge comments on the evidence to the jury, the judge must also advise the jury that they are the sole finders of fact and they may reach a conclusion contrary to the judge's comments. If a judge improperly refers to the evidence, the attorney should make an appropriate objection to such a misstatement.

Example

Objecting Lawyer:

> Objection. We respectfully submit that your Honor has (improperly commented on the evidence, has improperly made remarks concerning the credibility of witnesses, and has improperly advised the jurors that you would never hire me to clean a stable let alone try a case.)

1.45 Preserving the Evidentiary Error

An evidentiary error is properly preserved if steps are taken to make a record of the error and to provide the judge with notice and an opportunity to correct the error or reduce its prejudicial impact. In most jurisdictions to preserve an evidentiary error for appeal, the attorney must:

Timely object on the record.

Specifically state all available grounds. The failure to state a ground usually waives the omitted ground, unless it is readily apparent from the context.

Include the evidentiary error in a motion for a new trial or hearing.

Raise the specific evidentiary issue on appeal.

If the error occurs as a result of a party or witness introducing inadmissible evidence, the opposing attorney must also request a curative or limiting instruction, and may make a motion to strike, if appropriate. If the objection is sustained, the examining attorney must make an offer of proof.

1.46 Motion for Mistrial

Inadmissible evidence that has been improperly admitted may be a ground for a mistrial. In court trials, arbitrations and administrative hearing new trials or hearings are rarely granted. The judges believe they can separate out and ignore inadmissible evidence. In a jury trial, the inadmissible evidence must be so unfairly prejudicial that a party is denied a fair trial because of the impact of the evidence on the minds of the jurors. Usually, a curative instruction is sufficient to reduce the impact of inadmissible evidence. If the impact of some evidence cannot be cured by an instruction, a mistrial may be granted.

Example

Objecting Lawyer:

> Objection, your Honor. Counsel has referred to evidence that your Honor previously ruled inadmissible. I now move for a mistrial on the grounds that this misconduct is so unfairly prejudicial that my client is denied a fair trial. A curative instruction will not remove from the minds of the jurors what they

have heard. This inadmissible and highly prejudicial information that has been presented prevents them from considering the evidence in a fair and impartial manner. Furthermore, I ask that the court admonish counsel for such improper misconduct, and wash counsel's mouth out with bar soap.

1.47 Prejudicial Error

In order for an evidentiary error to be a prejudicial (reversible) error, the error a judge makes must adversely affect a substantial right of a party. Many evidentiary rulings are incorrect, but only amount to "harmless error." Harmless error in an evidentiary situation is an error that does not substantially prejudice a party. Most evidentiary errors during a trial or hearing are harmless and not sufficiently prejudicial to warrant a new trial or reversal. If an error of great magnitude occurs and the attorney fails to object, the "plain error" doctrine permits the appellate court to reverse a decision based on an error that is obvious and that adversely affects substantial rights of a party.

1.48 Appellate Review

Appellate courts do not often reverse incorrect evidentiary rulings. An appellate court is more likely to reverse an evidentiary ruling if a judge excludes evidence, than when the judge admits the evidence. The appellate courts reason that the exclusion of this evidence from consideration by the fact finder may deny a party a substantial right to a trial based on relevant, reliable evidence. Consequently, judges, in ruling on close evidentiary issues, are more inclined to admit rather than exclude evidence.

CHAPTER 2
EVIDENTIARY
OBJECTIONS

A. OBJECTIONS TO DIRECT EXAMINATION
QUESTIONS

This section explains common objections to the improper form of questions asked on direct examination. The cross-examiner can use these objections to force the direct examiner to ask proper questions. Some of these objections may apply to questions asked on cross-examination.

2.01 Leading Questions

Generally, asking leading questions during direct examination is improper. Fed.R.Evid. 611. Leading questions are questions that suggest the answer. The problem with leading questions is that the attorney is testifying instead of the witness. Leading questions are permitted in limited situations during direct examination. Leading questions are permitted on cross-examination, unless, in some jurisdictions, the witness is clearly sympathetic and supportive of the party represented by the cross-examiner.

Usually a leading question is one that can be answered by a "yes" or "no" or a specific one or two word answer contained in that question. However, not all questions that call for "yes" or "no" or a short specific answer are leading. In order for a question to be leading, it must also suggest the answer to the witness. Even if leading questions are asked, there may not be any tactical advantage in objecting to them. Leading questions are often ineffective on direct examination because the fact finder does not hear the witness testify about the facts, since the lawyer is telling the story and the witness is merely affirming the lawyer's testimony.

Example

Examining Attorney:

Q: Mr. Frost, when the two roads diverged in a yellow wood, you took the one less traveled by, right?

Objecting Lawyer:

Objection, your Honor. Leading question.

Judge:

Sustained.

Responses to Objection:

Rephrase the question and ask a non-leading question.

Explain to the judge that the leading question falls within one of the permissible uses of leading questions on direct examination.

Explain to the judge that you are trying to speed the trial up by asking a reasonable number of leading questions. Judges sometimes prefer efficiency over the rules of evidence.

Advise the judge that you are much more credible than your witness.

2.02 Narrative Answer

An objection may be made to a question that calls for a narrative answer or to an answer that turns into a narrative. Fed.R.Evid. 611. An improper narrative question allows the witness to tell a long, uncontrolled story. For example, "In your own words, Mr. Jefferson, tell the jury everything that happened to you on July 4." Narrative questions allow the witness to interject inadmissible testimony without giving the opposing attorney a reasonable opportunity to object in a timely manner. Sometimes a witness will give a narrative response to an otherwise permissible question. A narrative answer may be objected to as being a narrative answer or as being non-responsive. As a tactical consideration, however, the attorney may not want to object to a witness' narrative if the "rambling" testimony tends to make the opponent's direct examination ineffective.

A narrative answer is improper because our adversary system requires specific answers to specific questions and not narrative answers to broad questions. A judge has discretion to sustain or overrule a narrative objection and will consider the scope of the question, the timing of the question, the apparent preparation of the witness, the ability of the witness to be responsive, and the ability of the attorney to control the examination. During a trial, seemingly objectionable narrative questions will be allowed because the judge realizes the witness will only give a brief response and the attorney can control the examination. For example, the attorney may ask the witness "Then what happened?" This question, if literally answered, would permit the witness to provide a narrative response explaining everything that happened. A well-prepared witness will ordinarily give a short response, and the examining attorney will follow up with a responsive question, such as "Then what happened after you arrived at the Temple?"

Example

Examining Attorney:

Q: Ms. Tiger, what happened as you pushed your shopping cart down the cereal aisle at Ortiz's market?

A: I went to the center left aisle to pick up my six-year-old's favorite cereal. When I reached for a box of Frosted Flakes, my right foot suddenly slid sideways. I kept sliding. I didn't notice the slippery floor. My ankle turned, and I fell down

on my right hip. I couldn't move. I felt
nauseated. I then saw the wet spots on the
floor. Everything went black and white. I closed
my eyes. I heard people talking, but I couldn't
look up to answer. When I looked up, there was
a cast on my right leg and an IV in my arm, and
I felt . . .

Objecting Lawyer:

Objection. Improper narration.

Judge:

Sustained.

Responses to Objection:

Politely interrupt the witness and stop the rambling.

Ask a specific question to maintain control of the direction
of the examination.

Explain to the judge that these open-ended questions save
time.

Explain that the narrative answers cover uncontroverted,
preliminary, or insignificant matters and do not cover
significant issues in the case.

Say to the witness: "I will now ask you some specific questions to which you can give specific answers."

During a recess, advise the witness to listen to and answer
the precise question, or you will go on strike.

2.03 Non-Responsive/Volunteered Answer

A non-responsive or volunteered answer occurs when a
witness provides information not required by the attorney's question. Any response that extends beyond the specific
information required is objectionable. Fed.R.Evid. 611. Some
authorities believe that only the examining attorney can make
this objection. In practice, however, the vast majority of judges
will sustain an opposing lawyer's objection if the witness on
direct examination testifies in a non-responsive manner.

⋅ Example

Examining Attorney:

Q: Ms. Leary, when did you become a maintenance manager?

A: Well, I had three brothers, and I was the only girl in the family after Mom died. The whole time we were growing up, I was competing with the guys. They were always fixing cars and working on engines and motors, mowing, painting, and doing things like that. It all looked like fun; so I tried to keep up, and I learned how to do those things right along with them . . .

Objecting Lawyer:

Objection. Witness is non-responsive.

Judge:

Sustained. Please just answer the question asked of you.

Responses to Objection:

Interrupt the witness politely and stop the non-responsive answer.

Ask more specific questions which require the witness to give shorter answers.

Take the witness out in the hallway and remind them who is at least nominally in charge of the case.

2.04 Vague and Ambiguous Questions

A question should be clear and understandable so that the witness can understand what is being asked. Vague and ambiguous questions are subject to objections. Fed.R.Evid. 611. Questions may be vague as to the time and circumstances of an event, or may be ambiguous in the choice of words used.

There may not be a tactical advantage to objecting to vague and ambiguous questions asked on direct examination if the testimony is confusing and not persuasive. An objection to a vague and ambiguous question may only assist the direct examiner in making clear something that is being presented in a confusing manner. The better tactic may be not to object but to allow the fact finder to remain confused.

Example

Examining Attorney:

    Q: Socrates, who attended your class?

Objecting Lawyer:

    Objection. Vague and ambiguous. The witness has taught different classes in Athens and Thermopolis.

Judge:

    Sustained.

Responses to Objection:

Rephrase the question to make it clearer.

Ask the witness if the question was understood.

If the objection is overruled, request that the court reporter read back the question to show how clear the question was and how opposing counsel is attempting to interrupt a proper examination.

Admit that you are equally uncertain about what you are asking.

2.05 Cumulative Evidence

Cumulative evidence is repetitious evidence. Fed.R.Evid. 403 and 611. Evidence is cumulative when a series of witnesses testify to the same thing or when a series of exhibits provide identical information. If the evidence is important, however, more witnesses or exhibits may relate to the same facts without being cumulative. But when many witnesses testify to the same event or when many nearly identical exhibits are offered, they serve no useful purpose and are therefore cumulative. Cumulative evidence is objectionable because it is repetitive, boring and unnecessary, like this sentence.

Example

Examining Attorney:

> The defense calls Citizen Kane.

Objecting Lawyer:

> Your Honor, I believe that counsel, through Citizen Kane, is trying to introduce more evidence of the plaintiff's alleged bad faith. This evidence is unnecessarily cumulative as this is the fourth witness testifying to the same thing.

Examining Attorney:

> Your Honor, we have a right to prove up our counterclaim based on the plaintiff's bad faith in bringing this action.

Judge:

> I will overrule the objection. The defense may introduce this evidence of the plaintiff's intent to intimidate and harass in bringing the lawsuit. However, this is the last witness you may call on this point.

Responses to Objection:

> Explain to the judge that this evidence is not repetitive, but adds important details to evidence already admitted.

> Explain to the judge that the evidence is not improperly cumulative. Rather, the corroborative evidence from additional sources is needed to buttress the facts being proved.

> If the objection is sustained, continue on with the questioning and return to the evidence during a later stage of the witness' examination.

> Explain that the evidence is not anywhere near as repetitious as was law school.

2.06 Misstatement of Evidence

Misstatement or mischaracterization of evidence is objectionable because it inaccurately describes evidence. Fed.R.Evid. 611. This objection may be used to object to responses by witnesses as well as questions. A misstatement or mischaracterization of evidence may be done inadvertently or intentionally. An opposing attorney or witness may not remember exactly what was said in previous testimony or the characterization may be a description of a piece of evidence that can be described with more than one term. For example, a letter opener may arguably be referred to as a knife-like object. Whether the problem is caused inadvertently or intentionally, an objection should be asserted and the judge should be requested to instruct the opposing attorney or witness to make proper reference to the evidence or testimony.

Example

Examining Attorney:

Q: What kind of meals did you receive while you worked on the ranch, Mr. Cartwright?

A: They were like poison. My father doled out stale sandwiches and watery soup as though we were prisoners of war.

Objecting Lawyer:

Objection. The witness is mischaracterizing the evidence. I request the judge to disregard that answer and the witness be instructed to properly answer the question.

Judge:

Objection sustained. I will disregard that answer. The witness is directed to answer the question and not to add unnecessary and improper descriptions.

Responses to Objection:

Point out to the court that evidence has already been introduced that refers to the question or answer.

Explain to the court that there is a source of evidence that will be introduced which will support this question or answer. Request that the court conditionally accept the answer subject to the introduction of supportive evidence.

Explain that the characterization in the question or answer is a proper admissible opinion.

Explain that the characterization by the witness is the way this witness ordinarily talks and expresses facts.

Get another character to be the witness.

2.07 Assuming Facts Not in Evidence

This objection is used to object to questions that assume facts that have not been introduced in evidence. See Fed.R.Evid. 611. A direct examiner who faces this objection may revise the question to eliminate the assumption of fact or may tell the judge that the assumed fact will be proven later. If the latter course is taken, the assumed fact must be proven. If that fact is not proven later, the opposing attorney may request that the fact finder disregard such evidence.

Example

Examining Attorney:

Q: Ms. Penelope, when did your husband, Mr. Ulysses, begin his search for you?

Objecting Lawyer:

Objection. There has been no evidence introduced about any search.

Judge:

Sustained.

Responses to Objection:

> Revise the question to bring out the questionable facts.
>
> If the witness can describe the facts, allow the witness to testify to the facts.
>
> Stop making things up.

B. OBJECTIONS TO CROSS–EXAMINATION QUESTIONS

This section explains common objections to improper questions asked on cross-examination. The direct examiner can use these objections to protect the witness from being asked improper questions. While some of these same objections may also be available during direct examination, the examples in this section illustrate cross-examination situations.

2.08 Repetitious Questions

If a question has been asked and answered, an attorney may object to similar questions as repetitious. Fed.R.Evid. 403 and 611. This objection prevents the opposing attorney from gaining undue advantage by repeating testimony. The form of the questions does not have to be absolutely identical in order to raise this objection. This objection is available during both direct and cross examination. This objection is also referred to as "asked and answered."

Example

Examining Attorney:

Q: Mr. Hur, at the time you purchased this chariot, Mr. Spartacus handed you a written warranty, didn't he?

A: Yes.

Q: And you had an opportunity to read that warranty over, didn't you?

A: Yes.

Q: And Mr. Spartacus explained to you the length of that warranty so that you understood how long the warranty would run, didn't you?

A: Yes.

Q: So, there was no question in your mind that you understood the length of time of that warranty, isn't that correct, Mr. Hur?

Objecting Lawyer:

Objection, your Honor. Repetitious.

Judge:

The objection is sustained.

Responses to Objection:

Explain that the point needs to be emphasized on cross-examination.

Explain that the witness is attempting to be evasive, thus requiring similar and related questions to pin the witness down.

Move on to the next line of questioning and emphasize this point during summation.

2.09 Misleading or Confusing Questions

A question must be reasonable, clear, and specific so that the witness knows what is being asked. Fed.R.Evid. 403.

Example

Examining Attorney:

Q: Mr. Quixote, since you ran away, you don't know whether Sancho did a good job or not, do you?

Objecting Lawyer:

Objection, your Honor, the words "good job" are vague and ambiguous.

Judge:

>   The objection is sustained.

Responses to Objection:

>   Ask if the witness understands the question.

>   Rephrase the question so it is not misleading or confusing.

2.10 Multiple or Compound Questions

A multiple or compound question presents two or more questions within a single question. These types of questions are objectionable because the answer will usually be ambiguous. Fed.R.Evid. 403 and 611.

Example

Examining Attorney:

>   Q: On the day of the alleged threat to Caesar's life, you talked to Brutus about Caesar's gladiator training, not the threat, and then you visited the defendant at his villa the same night to talk about minting new coins, didn't you?

Objecting Lawyer:

>   Objection, your Honor. Counsel is asking Mr. Augustus two questions at the same time.

Judge:

>   Sustained.

Responses to Objection:

>   Repeat one of the questions and ask the witness to answer that question and then ask the other question.

2.11 Mischaracterization of Evidence

This objection is often used to object to questions on cross-examination that include facts that are not in evidence or statements that improperly misstate or mischaracterize the evidence. Fed.R.Evid. 611. The improper or mischaracterized statement may be an attempt to trick the witness and may also be an argumentative question.

Example

Examining Attorney:

Q: Mr. Newton, when you stood under the tree a kumquat hit you on your foot, correct?

Objecting Lawyer:

Objection. There are no facts to support these inaccurate assumptions.

Judge:

Sustained.

Responses to Objection:

Introduce appropriate supporting evidence before asking this question. Laying a foundation makes this objection inappropriate.

Explain that evidence has been introduced which supports the question and refer the judge to such evidence.

Explain to the court that such evidence will be introduced at a later stage of the trial, and request that the judge conditionally accept this evidence subject to subsequent proof.

Argue that one of the purposes of cross is to test the memory and credibility of a witness and that the witness can deny the asserted facts if the witness disagrees with the assertion.

2.12 Argumentative Questions

Any question that is essentially an argument is improper. Fed.R.Evid. 611. The role of the attorney is to question and not to argue. An argumentative question either elicits no new information or harasses the witness. Argumentative questions often assume a sarcastic tenor: "Do you mean to tell me . . ." or "Doesn't it seem strange that . . . ."

Example

Examining Attorney:

Q: Matthew Starl, had you been keeping a proper look out, you must realize you would never have recklessly run over Lassie.

Objecting Lawyer:

I object to counsel arguing his case through this witness.

Judge:

Objection sustained. The jury will disregard counsel's statement.

Responses to Objection:

Re-ask the question and eliminate the objectionable comment.

Re-ask the question and change the tone so the question does not sound argumentative.

2.13 Improper Impeachment

Improper impeachment is an attempt to incorrectly discredit a witness. Fed.R.Evid. 613. Improper impeachment may occur in a variety of ways. A cross-examiner may attempt to impeach the witness on a collateral, unimportant, or irrelevant matter, or may attempt to impeach the witness with a prior statement that is not materially inconsistent.

Example

Examining Attorney:

Q: Mr. Daedalus, in a prior statement you said that Icarus was wearing wings made of yellow wax, not golden wax, true?

Objecting Lawyer:

Objection, your Honor. The color of the wax is not inconsistent, and this impeachment effort is improper.

Judge:

> Sustained.

Responses to Objection:

> Explain how the impeachment is not collateral or is materially inconsistent.

> Ask additional cross-examination questions to establish the relevancy and importance of the impeachment.

2.14 Beyond the Scope

Any questions that go beyond the permissible scope of an examination are objectionable. Fed.R.Evid. 611. Cross-examination is limited to the subject matter of the direct examination and matters relating to the witness' credibility. Credibility usually permits a broad range of questions. If the cross-examiner wishes to go beyond the permitted scope of the direct, the cross-examiner must usually call the witness and ask questions on direct examination. The cross-examiner may raise new matters, however, if the court permits. Many judges view the scope of cross-examination liberally and permit wide-ranging examinations as long as the questions are relevant to the case. A redirect examination may not go beyond the scope of a cross-examination. The redirect examination may not repeat the direct examination but may only clarify or cover new information raised by the cross-examination. A cross-examination is limited to new evidence brought out during the recross-examination.

Example

Examining Attorney:

> Q: Ms. Ingalls-Wilder, you later lived in a little house in Minnesota, didn't you?

Objecting Lawyer:

> Objection, your Honor. The question goes beyond the scope of the direct examination which was limited to the cabin in Wisconsin.

Judge:

> Sustained.

Responses to Objection:

> Point out the testimony from direct examination which relates to this question on cross-examination. The attorney may need to remind the judge about the question or answer on direct examination that touched on the subject. If an objection to the scope of cross-examination is anticipated, listen carefully during the direct examination for a related topic so that the judge can be shown that this topic or a related topic was asked during direct examination.

> Explain that the questions relate to the credibility of the witness or another witness.

> Explain to the court that the judge has substantial discretion to allow questions to be asked beyond the scope of direct examination.

> Explain to the judge that if these questions are not permitted at this stage of the trial, the witness will be recalled at a later stage which will only take more time and cause inconvenience to the witness.

C. OBJECTIONS BASED ON THE
EXCLUSIONARY RULES OF EVIDENCE

The exclusionary rules of evidence can be grouped into several categories:

> Irrelevant and unfairly prejudicial evidence.

> Privileged information.

> Lack of personal knowledge and improper opinion.

> Lack of foundation for documents and other exhibits.

Constitutional limitations on evidence in criminal cases.

Hearsay.

2.15 Irrelevant Evidence

Evidence must be relevant in order to be admissible. Relevant evidence has probative value, which is the tendency to make more or less probable any facts of consequence to the outcome of the case. Relevant evidence may be excluded when the probative value of that evidence is outweighed by its unfairly prejudicial effects. Fed.R.Evid. 401-403.

Relevant evidence may be either direct or circumstantial. Direct evidence is that which is proved by witnesses who testify to what they saw, heard, or experienced, or by physical evidence of the fact itself. Circumstantial evidence is that which can be reasonably inferred from other facts proven in the case. Most relevancy objections involve circumstantial evidence that requires the drawing of inferences that are weak or remote.

What is or is not relevant depends upon the particular evidence and the issues of each case. In offering evidence, an attorney must have an explanation for the evidence's relevance supporting its admissibility. In planning to introduce evidence, the attorney must consider what issue the evidence supports.

After a relevancy objection is made, the judge may or may not ask the examining attorney about the relevancy of the evidence, depending upon whether or not the relevancy is apparent in the context of the case. If the attorney can explain a connection between an issue in the case and the evidence offered, the judge will be inclined to overrule the objection. If the offering attorney anticipates that the judge may sustain the objection, the attorney may ask to be heard before the judge rules and explain the relevancy to the judge. If the objection is sustained, the offering attorney should make an offer of proof and explain the relevancy to the judge, which may change the judge's mind.

Judges often defer to the judgment of the attorney if the judge believes the attorney has properly planned the introduction of evidence. If the attorney can immediately explain to the judge the reasons supporting the relevancy of the evidence, the judge will more likely overrule an objection. If an attorney hesitates in explaining why a piece of evidence is relevant, the judge may believe that the attorney does not know why the evidence is being offered or has not properly prepared for trial.

Example

The defendant, James Moriarty, is identified as the robber of a convenience store. The owners have testified that the store was robbed at 9:45 a.m. The robber wore a neon green jogging suit. A resident of an apartment building one block from the store identified the defendant as the man who ran past her building at 9:45 a.m. wearing a neon green running suit.

Objection: Irrelevant.

Ruling: Overruled. The identification of defendant is admissible. The close proximity in time between the robbery and the neighbor's observation has a tendency to prove through circumstantial evidence that the defendant was the robber running from the store.

2.16 Immaterial Evidence

Evidence is material if it has some logical relationship to the case. Materiality has been subsumed by Federal Rules of Evidence 401 and 402 and similar state rules. The concept of materiality relates to the concept of what is of "consequence" to a case. What is of consequence depends on the scope of the pleadings, the theories of the case, and the substantive law. Materiality is included in an objection based on relevancy, and is no longer recognized as a distinct objection in most jurisdictions because immaterial evidence is almost always irrelevant.

Example

Plaintiff Cinderella seeks to prove that the defendant's improper maintenance of a stairway also contributed to the falls of two other residents of the defendant's apartment building. The other accident victims were hurt when they caught their heels in loose carpeting and tripped.

Objection: Irrelevant.

Ruling: Admissible if plaintiff shows that all the relevant circumstances were substantially identical to her own accident: the accidents all occurred on the same stairway, the same carpeting was in the same loose condition, the same means of securing the carpeting to the stairs was used, and the lighting conditions and other circumstances were the same.

2.17 Unfairly Prejudicial Evidence

Relevant evidence is inadmissible when its prejudicial effect substantially outweighs its probative value. The key to a successful assertion of an objection based on prejudicial evidence is that the evidence is unfairly prejudicial. All evidence is prejudicial in the sense that it hurts one party and helps the other party. Only evidence that is unfairly prejudicial may be excluded. This objection may be made against evidence that appeals to the passion or prejudice of the fact finders, to exhibits that unnecessarily display injuries, or to an event or a scene described in overly graphic or gruesome detail.

Inadmissible prejudicial evidence include the following categories specifically barred by the Federal Rules of Evidence and similar state rules of evidence.

2.17.1 Improper Character Evidence

The general rule is that evidence of a person's character traits are not admissible to prove that the person acted in conformity with those traits on a particular occasion. For example, evidence that the accused has stolen things in the past should not be allowed to prove that the accused stole money on a latter occasion. If character evidence is introduced in situations other than those permitted by the rules, an objection should be made. If character evidence is introduced by an improper method, an objection to the way the evidence is being introduced should be made. Fed.R.Evid. 404 and 405.

Example

Doctor Afuhruhurr is accused of medical malpractice for transplanting plaintiff's brain. Plaintiff's attorney presents evidence that Doctor Afuhruhurr is an arrogant, uncaring, overly demanding, and rude physician.

Objection: Unfairly prejudicial. Improper character evidence.

Ruling: Sustained.

This evidence of the doctor's character is not admissible to prove the doctor's negligence in the civil case. The doctor may be an arrogant and rude physician, but that information is unfairly prejudicial because the jurors may be influenced improperly and find the doctor negligent in this case because of the doctor's bad general character.

2.17.2 Improper Habit Evidence

Improper habit evidence is inadmissible. Fed.R.Evid. 406. An objection should be made as evidence of improper habits is being introduced. An example of an improper "habit" that is usually excluded involves evidence of intemperance. Evidence of excessive drinking is ordinarily inadmissible to prove drunkenness in accident cases. Similarly, evidence of other assaults is usually inadmissible in a civil assault case. These types of evidence are usually deemed inadmissible because they are unfairly prejudicial. The fact finder may be unfairly inclined to find the party guilty or liable because of past conduct and not decide the case based on the facts of the present case.

Example

Plaintiff testified that the defendant, Cameron, backed his car out of Ferris Bueller's driveway without looking, and ran into Plaintiff's car. Cameron claimed that he didn't see Plaintiff's car before he backed out because Plaintiff was speeding. Cameron's witnesses would testify the defendant periodically drove them to school, and he usually looked both ways before backing up.

Objection: Improper habit evidence.

Ruling: Sustained. This testimony is inadmissible evidence of habit. There is insufficient evidence to establish Defendant's looking both ways as a matter of habit.

2.17.3 Subsequent Remedial Measures

The term "subsequent remedial measures" refers to actions taken after an event which, if taken before the event, would have made the event less likely to occur. Fed.R.Evid. 407. An example is fixing a car's brakes after an accident caused by faulty brakes. Evidence of subsequent remedial measures is not admissible to prove negligence or fault in a previous event. Such evidence is considered to be unfairly prejudicial and misleading because the repairs inaccurately imply a recognition of liability or may divert attention from the real cause of the accident. For example, evidence that a railroad installed a crossing gate and warning lights after an accident should not be admissible to prove the railroad's fault because, in hearing the evidence, one might incorrectly infer that the railroad admitted it was negligent. If this type of evidence were admissible to prove fault, many types of repairs would not be made for fear that liability would be imposed on the person making repairs. The exclusion of subsequent remedial measures does not apply where the issue to be proved involves controverted matters of ownership, control, feasibility of precautionary measures, or impeachment of a witness. These reasons make subsequent remedial measures admissible in many cases.

Example

Plaintiff Sonja Henje slipped on the ice outside of Defendant's business. Defendant had received several previous complaints about the slippery conditions outside, but claimed that it would be too expensive to make the sidewalk safe. After Plaintiff's accident, Defendant bought a bag of de-icer for $5 and spread it on the ice, making it safe.

Objection: Unfairly prejudicial evidence.

Ruling: Sustained if offered to show Defendant's fault, but overruled if introduced to show feasibility of precautionary measures.

2.17.4   Offers of Compromise

Evidence of offers to resolve a dispute or attempts to settle a matter are not admissible, because the evidence might be misinterpreted as an admission of liability. Fed.R.Evid. 408. Parties are encouraged to negotiate and settle cases, and all statements, discussions, and admissions made during settlement talks are excluded from evidence. However, evidence of a compromise offer to prove bias of a witness or to rebut a contention of undue delay may be admitted as an exception to the general rule.

Example

Mr. Ferrari and Mr. Porsche were involved in an automobile accident where Mr. Ferrari's fender was dented. Each party believed the other was at fault, and an argument ensued. Mr. Porsche didn't want the hassle of going to court and gave Mr. Ferrari some money to fix his car. A few months later Mr. Ferrari developed some health problems that he claims were caused by the accident. Mr. Ferrari sued Mr. Porsche for personal injury, and attempted to present evidence at trial that the defendant paid for the plaintiff's damaged car after the accident.

Objection: Unfairly prejudicial evidence.

Ruling: Sustained. Defendant's payment to fix plaintiff's car might be interpreted as an admission of liability for the accident, and for plaintiff's later health problems.

2.17.5   Payment of Medical Expenses

Evidence of payment, promises to make payment, or offers to make payment for medical expenses by the opposing party may not be offered to prove liability for an injury. Fed.R.Evid. 409.

2.17.6   Plea Bargains

A person accused of a criminal offense may offer to plead guilty to a lesser offense rather than plead not guilty and go to trial. The person may also decide to plead nolo contendere, which means that the person neither admits nor denies guilt, but agrees that if the case went to trial there would be sufficient evidence for a finding of guilt. Offers to plead guilty to a lesser offense and pleas of nolo contendere are not admissions of guilt, and may not be used as evidence against the person in a later action. Once a guilty plea is accepted and entered by the court, the guilty finding may be admissible under very limited circumstances. If a guilty plea is entered and later withdrawn, however, it becomes inadmissible. Fed.R.Evid. 410.

2.17.7   Liability Insurance

The existence or nonexistence of insurance coverage is not admissible regarding an issue of negligence or wrongful actions. Evidence regarding insurance is admissible if offered to prove issues of agency, ownership, control, bias, or impeachment. Fed.R.Evid. 411.

2.17.8   Religious Beliefs or Opinions

Evidence of a person's religious beliefs or opinions is not admissible to show that the person is more or less credible. Fed.R.Evid. 610.

2.18 Privileged Communication

A privileged communication consists of a communication between persons having a confidential relationship. The policy behind the privilege is to encourage open, honest communication between certain persons. A valid objection based on privilege will bar the underlying communication from being disclosed. Fed.R.Evid. 501.

Common privileges include: attorney/client, doctor/patient, spousal communications, clergy/penitent, trade/business secrets, and news sources. Local statutes and case law must be consulted to determine available privileges in a jurisdiction. Every privilege has a number of elements that must be proved. The privilege may not be successfully asserted unless evidence is introduced to show the existence of these elements.

2.18.1 Attorney/Client Privilege

The establishment of an attorney/client privilege requires:

(1) A professional relationship between an attorney and a client who seeks legal advice, involving

(2) A communication made in confidence

(3) Between an attorney (or agent of the attorney) and client, who is the holder of the privilege.

2.18.2 Doctor/Patient Privilege

The establishment of a doctor/patient privilege requires:

(1) A doctor/patient relationship in which the patient seeks medical assistance, involving

(2) A communication regarding medical information, including examinations, reports, x-rays, and notes, made

(3) Between a doctor (or medical assistant) and a patient, who is the holder of the privilege.

2.18.3 Marital Communications Privilege

A limited privilege recognized in most jurisdictions protects confidential communications made between spouses during marriage. Neither spouse can testify, during or after marriage, concerning certain communications made between the spouses while married. Both spouses are holders of the privilege.

The establishment of a marital communication privilege requires:

(1) A marriage relationship, involving

(2) Confidential, private communications

(3) Made during the marriage.

2.18.4 Waiver of Privilege

Any privilege may be waived if:

> The holder or attorney, with the consent of the holder, knowingly and expressly waives the privilege;

> Voluntary disclosure of the privileged information occurs during discovery or trial testimony;

> No objection is made to a question eliciting privileged communications;

> A privileged matter is discussed in the presence of a third person;

> An eavesdropper without using surreptitious means, overhears a privileged communication; or

> The holder raises a claim or defense that places the privileged matter in issue.

If a privilege has been waived, an objection asserting the existence of a privilege will be overruled.

D. FOUNDATION OBJECTIONS

2.19 Lack of Personal Knowledge/Improper Opinion

A witness must be competent to testify. Competency embodies four factors: an understanding of the oath or affirmation, the perception of events, the recollection of those events, and the ability to communicate. Fed.R.Evid. 601–602.

Generally, a witness is presumed competent to testify unless challenged by the opponent or the court on its own motion (which judges rarely do). Objections to the competency of a witness are usually made before a witness takes the stand. If a witness does not appear competent while testifying, the opposing attorney may object and "voir dire" the witness to establish that the witness is not competent because the witness does not understand the oath, did not perceive a relevant event, does not remember the event, or cannot communicate. Because witnesses are usually competent, opposing lawyers rely on cross-examination to reduce the weight of the witnesses' testimony.

Example

Witness saw an auto accident between a car and a van, and testified that the van was rounding a curve before the collision occurred.

Examining Attorney:

Q: How fast was the van moving?

Objecting Lawyer:

Objection. Your Honor, this witness is not competent to testify to the speed of the van. She did not see the van for a sufficient amount of time before the collision because it was out of her view as it rounded the curve.

Ruling: Sustained. Some judges would overrule the objection and allow the evidence in for what it is worth.

A witness may not testify to any matter unless evidence is introduced which is sufficient to support a finding that the witness has personal knowledge of the matter. If the proponent does not establish that the witness has personal knowledge of the matters about which the witness will testify, an objection should be interposed. Whenever a witness is about to testify, the opposing attorney should silently ask: "How does the witness know this information?" or "What is the source of the information the witness is about to give?" If the opposing attorney knows the witness has firsthand knowledge and the information is reliable, no objection ought to be made. If the opposing attorney believes the witness does not have firsthand knowledge or that the source of information is unreliable, an objection should be made. The proper objection is either lack of personal knowledge or lack of foundation.

Example

Examining Attorney:

Q: What happened in the fencing room?

A: I told D'Artagnan and Aramis that I no longer was going to be a Musketeer and then I left the room, and they continued to talk about . . . .

Objecting Lawyer:

Objection. Your Honor, the witness has no personal knowledge of what D'Artagnan and Aramis said after he left the room.

Judge:

Sustained.

2.20 Lack of Foundation

Foundation is preliminary information which must be established before some evidence is admissible. A lack of foundation objection is used to prevent the introduction of evidence or simply to force the opposing attorney to provide the missing element of foundation. Fed.R.Evid. 901–903.

Example

Examining Attorney:

Q: Mr. Toad, what happened to your car on the way home?

A: It broke down.

Q: What caused the car to break down?

Objecting Lawyer:

Objection. Lack of foundation.

Judge:

The objection is sustained.

If the objection does not keep the evidence out but actually forces the examining attorney to establish the missing element of foundation, it may be strategically inappropriate to object because the additional foundation may make the evidence appear more credible. This is usually true if the examining attorney can supply the missing foundation.

Example

Examining Attorney:

Q: Before your car broke down, Mr. Toad, what did you first notice?

A: I saw black smoke coming out of the engine compartment.

Q: What did you see next?

A: The hood of the engine blew off, and I saw it land about a hundred feet to the side of the car.

Q: Then what happened?

A: I heard this explosion and saw a huge ball of fire erupt from the engine compartment.

Q: What happened after you heard this explosion and saw this huge ball of fire erupt from the engine compartment?

A: The car broke down.

A better tactical approach in this instance may be to not object, but later argue that the proponent failed to prove the missing element, causation.

2.21　Lack of Expert Opinion

Expert opinion is admissible to provide conclusions or inferences beyond the abilities of the fact finder. Fed.R.Evid. 702–705. Experts can give opinion testimony after the judge determines that:

> The subject matter of the opinion is not one of common knowledge but one of scientific, technical, or other specialized knowledge.
>
> The opinion will assist the trier of fact to understand evidence or determine a fact in issue.
>
> The expert by way of knowledge, skill, experience, training, or education possesses sufficient expertise to render an opinion.
>
> The basis of the opinion is reliable and will assist the trier of fact.

An objection should be made if these four factors have not been met.

Example

Annie Oakley testifies that she is qualified as a ballistics expert and that on the basis of the tests conducted on the handgun found in William Cody's possession, it is her opinion, based upon her education, training, and experience in ballistics analysis, that the bullet that killed the buffalo was fired from Mr. Cody's gun.

Objection: Improper expert opinion.

Ruling: Overruled. Ballistics is a widely accepted area of expertise in the courts. The witness is qualified as an expert. And the expert opinion will help the fact finder.

2.22 Lack of Lay Witness Opinion

L ay witnesses may render opinions and conclusions if such statements are rationally based on the perception of the witness and helpful to a clear understanding or determination of a fact in issue. Fed.R.Evid. 701. Lay witnesses can render opinions if they have personal knowledge to support their perceptions and if there is a rational basis for the conclusion. There are many opinions and conclusions a lay witness may render. Permissible lay opinions may be given regarding speed, distance, time, appearances, conditions, emotions, age, health, sobriety, value of personal property, and other rational perceptions. Lay witnesses may testify that a person appeared nervous, happy, sad, scared, excited, or drunk. Inadmissible lay opinions are those that exceed the perception of the witness, are not rationally based, or do not assist the fact finder.

Lay witnesses may testify to a conclusion in some situations even though they are unable to explain specific observations that support the conclusion. The most common example involves the formation of an instantaneous opinion regarding matters that are observed, referred to as the collective facts doctrine. For example, an eye witness to an accident in which a pedestrian was hit by a car can testify to the conclusion that the car could not have swerved in time to avoid hitting the pedestrian. It would be difficult, if not impossible, for the witness to testify to specific, detailed facts that support the opinion. This type of conclusion assists in determining the facts and is admissible in most jurisdictions.

Example

Examining Attorney:

Q: What did you see, Mr. Leinenkugel?

A: I saw the defendant holding a can of beer in one hand
      and staggering as he walked over to me. His
      eyes were blood-shot, he smelled like a brewery,
      and he slurred his words.

Q: Describe his condition.

A: He was drunk.

Q: What else did you conclude?

A: He was negligent when he drove the car while drunk and he caused the accident.

Objecting Lawyer:

Objection. Improper opinion.

Judge:

Sustained. While the witness may testify that the defendant was drunk when he talked to him, the witness cannot draw the conclusion that the defendant was negligent because he did not perceive the event.

2.23 Speculation

Any question that asks the witness to guess or engage in conjecture is objectionable. Fed.R.Evid. 602 and 701. Speculation on the part of a witness as to what could have happened is usually of little probative value. Words like if, should, could, and similar phrases in a question may render a question susceptible to this objection.

Example

Examining Attorney:

Q: How close were you to Lancelot when he was knocked off his horse?

A: About fifteen feet away.

Q: Could Gwenivere have avoided Lancelot if she had been cantering instead of galloping her horse?

Objecting Lawyer:

Objection, the question calls for speculation.

Judge:

Sustained. The witness' opinion is speculative and has little probative value.

E. DOCUMENT OBJECTIONS

2.24 Admissibility of Documents

Four evidence rules determine the admissibility of a document:

> Relevancy.
>
> Hearsay.
>
> Original writing.
>
> Authentication.

Whenever a document is introduced, an opposing attorney should review the document for potential objections and determine whether these objections have been overcome by the attorney offering the document. Parts of a document may also be objectionable, and the attorney should scrutinize the entire document to make sure all the paragraphs, sentences, phrases, and words are admissible. If any one of these objections may preclude the introduction of part of a document, an objection should be made to exclude that portion of the document which is objectionable.

Example

Examining Attorney:

> Your Honor, Ms. Dickinson offers Plaintiff's Exhibit No. 640, the poem, as evidence.

Objecting Lawyer:

> I object, your Honor, to the admission of a part of this Exhibit. I object to the introduction of the handwritten notes in the margin of this document. There has been no foundation made to authenticate the handwriting, and this handwritten statement constitutes inadmissible hearsay.

Judge:

> Sustained. The handwritten notes in the left margin are excluded from evidence and are to be removed. The remainder of Plaintiff's Exhibit No. 640 is received into evidence.

2.25 Original Writings

The modern "original writings" rule permits originals and duplicate originals to be introduced to prove the contents of a writing, unless a question exists regarding the authenticity of the original or if it would be unfair to introduce a duplicate. Fed.R.Evid. 1001–1007. This rule is also known as the "best evidence" rule, which is a misleading term. The traditional "best evidence" rule required that the original of the document be introduced to prove its contents, and did not permit copies of the original. Modern evidence law recognizes that there may be a number of "originals" of a document and that mechanical reproduction machines or computer printers produce accurate and reliable duplicate originals. Documents covered by the original writings rule include all written documents, recordings, and photographs.

The modern rule specifically provides that duplicates are admissible to the same extent as an original unless there is a question about the authenticity of the original, or some other unfairness. The modern rule also provides that if neither the original nor a duplicate exist, if the original and copies have been inadvertently lost or destroyed, or if the documents cannot be obtained by any available judicial process or subpoena, other evidence of the contents of the writing is admissible. The "original writing" objection is usually sustained when the witness testifies about the substance or interprets a document.

Example

Examining Attorney:

Q: Ms. Morris, what did your lease set out as the rules about cats?

Objecting Lawyer:

> Objection. The original of the document must be introduced.

Judge:

> Sustained.

Some evidence that is written in a document may be admissible through oral testimony without the need to introduce the document. There are three specific situations where oral testimony provides accurate and reliable evidence without the need for the available document to be admitted.

(A) Signs, Labels, Tags

A witness may testify to the contents of a writing inscribed on a sign, label, or tag. Because there are only a few words on these items, the testimony is reliable. If an item contained a lengthy statement, then the original writing rule would apply. For example, a witness can testify that a sign read "no trespassing," but cannot testify regarding a sign containing several detailed sentences.

(B) Independent Facts

Facts that exist independently of a document and that are known to a witness may be established without requiring that the document be produced. For example, a witness may testify that a payment was made and not have to produce a canceled check or a copy of a paid bill. For another example, a tenant may testify to the amount and due date of the rent paid without having to produce the original lease. In these examples, the facts are independently known without reliance on the document because the witness paid or received the money. On the other hand, a written document is required to be introduced to establish facts that are not independent of the document, such as detailed terms or provisions.

(C) Collateral Matter

If the writing, recording, or photograph is collaterally (indirectly) related to the issue to be proved, and the need for producing the original is minimal, secondary evidence by way of oral testimony will be permitted. For example, if a witness testifies to a date that appears in a diary calendar, the original of the diary calendar need not be introduced if the actual date is not significant to the case.

2.26 Lack of Authentication

Writings must be authenticated to be admissible, that is, they must be shown to be what they purport to be. Fed.R.Evid. 901–902. Authentication is a foundational requirement for the introduction of writings. A lack of authentication objection is identical to a lack of foundation objection.

Example

In a copyright case, Shakespeare introduces a signed letter that he claims was written by Roger Bacon.

Objection: The letter is not authentic because there is no testimony that the signature of Roger Bacon is genuine and Mr. Bacon denies writing the letter.

Ruling: Sustained, unless Shakespeare offers evidence of authenticity.

2.27 Parol Evidence Rule

The parol evidence rule provides that a written agreement cannot be contradicted or modified by oral or written evidence of a prior or contemporaneous agreement. Exceptions to this rule occur when the contract is ambiguous, when the writing is not intended to be a complete and final expression of the agreement, or when fraud or mistake was committed in the formation of the contract.

Example

Phineas Fogg agreed to buy a hot air balloon from Jules Verne for $25,000. Verne said he would supply propane gas for one month without charge. Fogg and Verne signed a contract which stated that Fogg purchased the balloon for $25,000, but did not mention anything about the gas. When Fogg later attempted to obtain the propane gas, Verne told him he would have to pay for it. Fogg sued Verne, and Fogg now attempts to testify about the agreement for free fuel.

Objection: The parol evidence rule prohibits testimony contradicting or modifying a writing.

Ruling: Sustained. If the agreement regarding the gas was indeed part of this contract, it should have been in writing.

2.28 Constitutional Limitations in Criminal Cases

Evidence that may be reliable under the rules of evidence may be excluded in a criminal case because it was not obtained by the government in a fair way. Criminal constitutional exclusionary rules were developed by the federal and state courts to exclude evidence obtained in a way that violated the defendant's constitutional rights. For example, if evidence or statements were obtained from a defendant through an unconstitutional search or improper interrogation of the defendant by the police, they will not be admissible even though they would be admissible under the general rules of evidence.

CHAPTER 3
HEARSAY

A. HEARSAY EVIDENCE

3.01 Introduction to Hearsay

Hearsay is an out-of-court statement offered to prove the truth of the matter asserted. See Fed.R.Evid. 801. Hearsay occurs when a witness repeats an out-of-court statement. The out-of-court statement is made by a declarant, who can be either the testifying witness or another person. Hearsay is excluded because it involves one or more defects making it unreliable and untrustworthy:

> The fact finder has no opportunity to observe the credibility of the declarant when the statement was made, to gauge the sincerity, perception, or memory of the declarant, or to resolve ambiguities in the declarant's statement.

> The out-of-court statement may not be restated accurately because the witness may have misheard or misunderstood the statement.

> At the time the statement was made the declarant was not under oath.

> It may not be possible to cross-examine the declarant.

Most hearsay statements are admissible, either because the statements do not meet the legal definition of hearsay or because an exception provides for their admissibility.

Haydock,Bk 4 Advocacy --4

3.02 Hearsay Definition

There are three essential factors to a hearsay statement. If any one factor is absent, the statement is not hearsay.

The first factor is that the "statement" must be an oral or written assertion or nonverbal conduct intended to be an assertion. Hearsay statements may be oral, written, or asserted conduct. Oral testimony and written documents are hearsay statements, but not all conduct is a statement within the meaning of hearsay. Only assertive conduct constitutes hearsay. Assertive conduct is conduct that is intended by the actor to be an assertion. For example, during a line-up, the victim points her finger at the defendant. This is assertive nonverbal conduct. The statement implied in that conduct is "the defendant did it."

The second factor is that the statement must be an "out-of-court" statement. A hearsay statement is a prior statement made by a declarant outside the court or hearing room which is repeated by the witness in court or at a hearing. Three examples illustrate this factor:

> If the witness, Ichabod Crane, on the witness stand states, "Brom Bones said the horseman is headless," that statement is an out-of-court statement.

> If witness Ichabod Crane on the stand states, "I said the horseman is headless," that statement is also an out-of-court statement.

> If witness Ichabod Crane on the stand states, "I saw the Headless Horseman," that testimony is not hearsay.

The first two examples are out-of-court statements because they were made outside of the courtroom and were repeated in the courtroom. The third example is not a restatement of a prior statement, but a description of an event.

The third factor is that the out-of-court statement is offered to prove the truth of what the statement says. If the statement is offered for any other purpose, it is not hearsay. One way of determining whether the third factor has been met is to compare "what the statement proves" with "what the proponent is trying to prove." If there is a match, the statement is hearsay. If there is not a match, the statement is not hearsay. For example, a witness testifies that Mr. Black Elk said it was snowing on Mt. Rushmore on May 1. If the statement is offered to prove that it was actually snowing on Mt. Rushmore on May 1, the statement is hearsay. If the statement is offered to prove that the witness could identify the voice of Mr. Black Elk, the statement is not hearsay.

3.03 Admissible Out-of-Court Statements

Out-of-court statements that are admissible include:
    Statements not offered for the truth of the matter asserted.
    Nonassertive conduct.
    Non-propositions.
    Verbal acts.
    "Statements" by a declarant who is not a person.
    Party admissions.
    Prior statements by witnesses.
    Prior identification.

3.03.1 Statements Not Offered for the Truth of the Matter Asserted

As a general rule stated above, an out-of-court statement offered to prove the truth of the matter asserted is inadmissible hearsay. A statement offered to prove a fact other than the truth of the matter asserted may be admissible. For example, a witness overheard the groom, who is not a party in the matter, say "I do. I do." If offered for the truth of the matter asserted—that the groom consented—it is inadmissible hearsay. If offered for some other purpose, "I do. I do." is not hearsay. For example, if the statement is offered to prove that the groom was alive at the time the statement was made, it is not hearsay. If offered to prove the groom could talk, it is not hearsay. When offered for another purpose, the contents of the statement need not be believed for the evidence to be relevant. The mere fact that the statement was made—independent of its truth—is what is relevant and reliable.

A statement may appear to be offered for its truth but is primarily offered for another purpose. Common examples of such statements include statements offered to prove that an individual had notice or knowledge of something. For example, if a service station attendant tells a driver that his engine needs oil, that statement may be introduced at trial to determine a breach of warranty claim brought by the driver. The statement is introduced primarily to show that the driver had notice that the engine needed oil and not for the truth of the matter asserted.   •

3.03.2 Nonassertive Conduct

Nonassertive conduct—conduct not intended by the actor to stand for the matter to be proved—is not hearsay. For example, an issue at trial is whether it was cold and windy at an intersection, and Sherlock Holmes testifies that, "I observed from my window people standing at the intersection all faced in one direction, wearing heavy coats, with their collars upturned, and their hands in their pockets." The nonverbal conduct by the pedestrians is nonassertive conduct because they did not intend their acts to stand for the proposition sought to be proved at trial—that it was cold and windy. Nonassertive conduct is admissible because it is reliable.

3.03.3 Non-propositions

Statements are hearsay only if they contain a "proposition," that is, a statement that is offered for the truth of its contents. A common non-proposition statement is a question. Questions are usually not hearsay because they often do not contain any proposition. For example, a statement "I said, 'What did you say?' " is usually not hearsay, but the statement "I said, 'Daley, who is in Chicago with me?' " is hearsay because it contains a proposition that Daley is in Chicago.

3.03.4   Verbal Acts

Statements known as "verbal acts" or "operative words" are not considered hearsay because they are not offered for the truth of the matter asserted, but, rather, for their legal significance. The making of the statements creates legal duties or obligations irrespective of the truth asserted. The most common examples are statements which constitute the words of an offer or acceptance creating a contract, or defamatory words spoken to establish slander. For example, in a contract case, the witness can testify that "I heard the President say 'I will sell you this saxophone if you sell me those pork rinds.' " Further, in a defamation case, a witness can testify "Chambers said Hiss was a communist."

3.03.5   Declarant Not a Person

A statement is hearsay only if made by a person. A "statement" not made or produced by a person is not hearsay. A result produced by an inanimate object such as a machine or the conduct of an animal is not hearsay. For example, the number produced by a radar device which displays the speed of an automobile is not a hearsay statement; a dog that was trained to smell narcotics and who points to a package does not make a hearsay statement; a witness who testifies that her watch said "two-thirty" is not making a hearsay statement because the watch is not a person, and a statement by a raven who says "nevermore" is not hearsay.

3.03.6 Party Admissions

Any statement made by an opposing party or the party's agent, employee, or representative is admissible when offered against that party. Fed.R.Evid. 801(d)(2). An admission is defined as a statement made or an act done by a party to a lawsuit. A working definition of party admissions is: Anything an opposing party ever said or did that has anything to do with the case will be admissible. A plaintiff can testify to what a defendant said, and a defendant can testify to what the plaintiff said. A witness can testify to what any party said if offered by the opposing party against the declarant party.

Statements by an opposing party are admissible because the party should assume responsibility for statements made and because the party has a full opportunity to explain why the statement was made to place it in proper context. Admissions extend to statements made by agents, authorized persons, co-conspirators, and to adopted or approved statements made by other representatives of the party. For example, Casey, an engineer of defendant's train, tells an investigator, "The brakes did not work, and I was not looking where I was going." The investigator can be called by the plaintiff to repeat Casey's statements.

Party admissions are the major reason only statements made by the opposing party are admissible.

3.03.7 Prior Statements by Witnesses

Prior inconsistent statements made by witnesses under oath at a trial, hearing, deposition, or other proceeding are admissible as substantive evidence of the statements made. Fed.R.Evid. 801(d)(1). Prior consistent statements are admissible to rebut an indirect or express charge against the witness of recent fabrication, improper influence or motive. The declarant must testify at trial and be subject to cross-examination. The federal rules and similar state rules admit prior inconsistent statements in evidence as substantive proof. Some states only permit prior statements to be introduced for impeachment purposes and do not permit them to be considered by the fact finder as substantive proof.

For example, during a deposition, Paul Revere states "There was one lamp in the belfry arch." After the deposition, Paul Revere makes changes in his deposition testimony and now states "There were two lanterns in the belfry." During direct examination at trial, Paul Revere says "There were two lanterns in the belfry." On cross-examination, Paul Revere can be asked: "Prior to this trial, you stated that there was one lamp in the belfry arch." This statement is offered to prove the truth of the matter asserted—that there was only one lamp—and also offered to impeach the witness. During redirect examination, Paul Revere can testify that he said after the deposition that there were two lanterns. This statement is offered to corroborate the direct testimony and to rebut the impeachment by the prior inconsistent statement. In states that do not follow the federal rules, the prior statements are only admissible to impeach and to rebut impeachment and not to prove there was one lamp. Where is Wordsworth when you need him to rewrite this example so you don't have to re-read it?

3.03.8 Prior Identification

Prior identification of a person made by a witness after observing the person is admissible if the declarant testifies at trial and is subject to cross-examination. Fed.R.Evid. 801(d)(1). This rule allows a witness to testify to a prior identification statement made during or shortly after viewing the person or after identifying a photograph of the person.

For example, a witness, Cole Porter, who saw an assailant, tells the police that the assailant was "Five foot two with eyes of blue." At trial, Mr. Porter can say: "I told the police that the person who attacked me was five foot two with eyes of blue." Also at that trial, the police officer can state: "Mr. Porter told me that the suspect was five foot two with eyes of blue."

3.04 Hearsay Myths

A number of myths exist regarding hearsay. These myths arise from a misunderstanding of the application of the hearsay rules. An explanation of some of these myths may clear up some of the misperceptions regarding hearsay.

MYTH: All out-of-court statements are inadmissible hearsay. Most out-of-court statements are admissible.

MYTH: A witness on the stand can testify to whatever the witness has said in the past.

A witness on the stand who repeats what he or she has said in the past is testifying to an out-of-court statement. Such testimony must be analyzed under the hearsay rules to determine admissibility. The declarant's mere presence on the stand does not automatically make any prior statements admissible.

MYTH: If a witness can be cross-examined, all prior statements of that witness are admissible.

Merely because a witness has testified or is available to be cross-examined does not automatically make all prior statements by that witness admissible. Out-of-court statements by that declarant must be analyzed to determine if they are admissible statements.

MYTH: If the proper foundation is laid to authenticate a relevant document, the document is admissible.

Authentic and relevant documents are admissible only if they contain admissible out-of-court statements. The contents of the document must comply with the hearsay rules to be admissible.

MYTH: <u>Affidavits (statements made under oath) are admissible.</u>

An affidavit, though made under oath, is a hearsay statement. An affidavit must satisfy a hearsay exception, such as past recollection recorded, to be admissible.

MYTH: <u>Affidavits are admissible if the witness is unavailable.</u>

An affidavit made by a person who is unavailable to testify is not an admissible substitute for the testimony of that person. Such an affidavit constitutes inadmissible hearsay.

MYTH: <u>Res gestae makes much of hearsay admissible.</u>

The phrase "res gestae" (which means "the things done") was created during the early development of hearsay exceptions, but has now been replaced by modern rules of evidence. The phrase means different things to different advocates, and is only recognized in a few jurisdictions. The use of the phrase should be limited to Latin classes.

MYTH: <u>Judges flip a coin when ruling on hearsay objections.</u>

Most judges base their ruling on the applicable hearsay rules. Some judges are inclined to overrule hearsay objections because of the unlikelihood that an appellate court would reverse their evidentiary ruling and grant a new trial. Some judges misunderstand or misapply the rules of hearsay and improperly overrule hearsay objections. Hearsay objections should, however, be made in an attempt to exclude unreliable evidence and to make a record for appeal.

MYTH: <u>After a hearsay statement has been admitted, little can be done about its impact.</u>

Even if questionable hearsay is allowed in, much can be done to reduce its effect. Cross-examination questions can demonstrate its unreliability, and the defects of the evidence can be pointed out during closing argument as a basis for why the hearsay ought not to be believed.

MYTH: <u>No one understands hearsay, so who cares?</u>

Ninety plus percent of the hearsay situations and rules are relatively easy to understand and apply. It is the remaining 1 to 10 percent that can drive an advocate to municipal bond practice. If one of those impossible-to-figure-out-situations arises, refer the case to a lawyer who got a high grade in evidence.

MYTH: <u>Hearsay is fun to learn and not at all frustrating.</u>

The most frustrating aspect of hearsay is that different judges and lawyers have different understandings of the hearsay rules, making this aspect of trial life ridden with anxiety. Hearsay can become a little less frustrating if the advocate develops an understanding of hearsay and hearsay exceptions, flexibly adapts to the view the judge has on hearsay, and offers evidence consistent with the judge's anticipated rulings.

MYTH: <u>There is always a hearsay exception that makes the hearsay statement admissible.</u>

A hearsay statement must meet the requirements of a hearsay exception to be admissible. There are a reasonable—but nonetheless limited—number of hearsay exceptions. Read on.

B. HEARSAY EXCEPTIONS

3.05 Say What?

Many hearsay statements are admissible because one or more exceptions to the hearsay rule make them admissible. Fed.R.Evid. 803–804. The federal rules of evidence have codified twenty-nine separate exceptions, and many states recognize more.

There are a number of policy reasons as to why these exceptions have been developed. A common reason is that the hearsay exceptions recognize that some hearsay statements are reliable and trustworthy. If the traditional defects of unreliability and untrustworthiness do not exist, the statement ought to be admissible. A second rationale supports those hearsay statements where the declarant can be cross-examined. If there is an opportunity to cross-examine the person who made the hearsay statement, it may be appropriate to allow that statement to be admitted. A third explanation is there is no efficient or economical way of proving the fact except through the hearsay statement. Some exceptions to the rule against hearsay have been created in part to respond to the pragmatic needs of introducing evidence.

The following sections explain the most commonly recognized hearsay exceptions. Most jurisdictions, including the federal system, divide hearsay exceptions into two general groups which depend upon the availability of the declarant to testify.

Hearsay statements which are excepted from the hearsay rule regardless of whether the declarant is available to testify include:

> Sense impressions,
>
> State of mind assertions,
>
> Records, and
>
> Reputation evidence.

Additional hearsay statements which are excepted from the hearsay rule *only when the declarant is unavailable to testify* include: former testimony, statements against interest, statements of personal or family history, and dying declarations.

In addition to these exceptions, some hearsay statements will be excepted from the rule if certain specific requirements of reliability are met. The federal rules and many state jurisdictions designate this exception as the "residual" exception.

3.06 Present Sense Impressions

Present sense impressions and statements describing or explaining an event or condition made while the declarant was perceiving the event or condition, or immediately thereafter. Fed.R.Evid. 803(1). This is a broad exception and covers many statements made by persons involved in or who observe an event. This exception has two specific requirements:

> The statement describes or explains an event or condition, and

> The statement is made immediately or shortly after the declarant perceives the event or condition.

These spontaneous statements are deemed reliable because of the lack of time for reflective thought which can result in a changed perception of the event, and because the witness is likely to have a fresh memory of the event at the time the statement was made.

Example

Bo Jangles falls on a dance floor and is injured. Mr. Jangles' attorney calls Ms. Cherise, a witness, to testify about Bo's accident.

Examining Attorney:

> Q: Where were you standing?

> A: I was standing next to Mr. Caruthers, and both of us were standing near Bo when he fell.

> Q: What did Mr. Caruthers say when Mr. Jangles fell?

Objecting Lawyer:

> Objection. Hearsay.

Judge:

> Overruled.

> A: Mr. Caruthers said to me "This dance floor is very slippery, I almost fell myself a moment ago."

> Q: What did you do next?

> A: I walked over, slowly, to help Bo.

> Q: What did Mr. Jangles say?

Objecting Lawyer:

> Objection. Hearsay.

Judge:

> Overruled.

A: He said "This floor has some slippery stuff on it."

Both objections are overruled because both declarants, Mr. Caruthers and Mr. Jangles, made statements about a condition immediately after perceiving the event. The statement by Mr. Jangles is not a party admission because it is not being offered against him, but rather is being offered on his behalf.

3.07 Excited Utterances

Statements made by the declarant while under stress or excitement caused by a startling situation, and which relate to that situation, are admissible as excited utterances. Fed.R.Evid. 803(2). This exception only applies if:

> The statement is made by the declarant while under stress,
>
> The declarant has personal knowledge of the event by participating in or observing the event,
>
> The statement is prompted by the startling event, and
>
> The statement relates to the event.

The rationale for this exception is that spontaneous statements made under stress or during a startling event are reliable because a person does not have time to fabricate such statements.

Many statements are both excited utterances and present sense impressions. An excited utterance statement differs from a present sense impression in two aspects. One, while an excited utterance usually occurs during or immediately after an event, it need not occur at those times. As long as the declarant is still upset by the event when the statement is made, it is an excited utterance. The present sense impression must be made at the time of the event or immediately thereafter. Two, the excited utterance need only "relate" to the startling event, while a present sense impression must "describe or explain" an event or condition.

Example

In a personal injury case, Jill witnesses a startling event and testifies at trial that she said, "Oh no, the handle of the pail cracked and Jack fell down and broke his crown!" The opposing lawyer, representing the manufacturer of the pail, anticipating Jill's response, would object to the statement as hearsay. The judge would overrule the objection because the statement is an excited utterance, and is also a present sense impression.

3.08 State of Mind or Body Exceptions

Statements by a declarant involving the declarant's existing state of mind, emotion, sensation, or physical condition (such as intent, plan, motive, design, mental feeling, pain, and bodily harm) are admissible. Fed.R.Evid. 803(3). These statements are reliable because of their spontaneous nature. They are made at the time the declarant experiences the mental, emotional, or physical condition.

Example

In a products liability case, a witness called by the plaintiff testifies that he heard the plaintiff, Knievel, state right after the jumping accident: "My head is throbbing. I got the chills. I feel depressed. I hate the guy who sold me this motorcycle. I am going to go back to the cycle store and complain." All these statements are admissible as statements of existing physical, emotional, and mental conditions.

This exception does not include statements of past conditions. For example, if Knievel also said: "Last week, my back hurt," the statement is inadmissible hearsay because it refers to a past condition. If Knievel also said: "My back hurts," the statement is admissible because it refers to a present, existing condition.

3.09 Medical Treatment Statements

Statements made by one person who describes medical history, past or present pains, or symptoms to a medical professional for purposes of medical diagnosis or treatment are admissible. Fed.R.Evid. 803(4). These statements are deemed reliable because the declarant who seeks medical treatment has little or no incentive to lie.

Example

In a personal injury accident, the plaintiff's treating physician is called to testify on behalf of the plaintiff.

Examining Attorney:

Q: When did you examine Mr. Lemon?

A: About two weeks after the accident.

Q: What did Mr. Lemon tell you about his injuries at that time?

Objecting Lawyer:

Objection. Hearsay.

Judge:

Overruled.

A: Mr. Lemon said that right after the accident his neck hurt a lot and that up until the day before he saw me he could not turn his head to the right or left.

Q: What else did he say about his injury?

Objecting Lawyer:

Objection. Hearsay.

Judge:

Overruled.

A: He said he had hurt his neck when his head hit the headrest.

Q: What else did he say about the cause of the injury?

Objecting Lawyer:

Objection. Hearsay.

Judge:

Sustained.

The first objection is properly overruled because the testimony consists of a medical diagnosis. The second objection is also properly overruled because the cause of the injury is a relevant part of the information the doctor needs to properly diagnose and treat the injury. The third objection is properly sustained because any further statement, such as "It was defendant's reckless driving that caused my neck injury," is not a part of the patient's medical history.

3.10 Records

Several hearsay exceptions permit the admissibility of specific categories of records. These records are deemed reliable because the information they contain is usually entered and maintained in an accurate, trustworthy manner.

Business records

Public records

Specific records

Absent records

Past recollection recorded

3.11 Business Records

Records kept in the ordinary, regular course of a business or other organization are admissible. Fed.R.Evid. 803(6). Records include memoranda, reports, data compilation, documents, or any other type of written information. Recorded information includes facts, opinions, and other information. The term "business" includes any business, institution, association, profession, occupation, and organization, whether profit or nonprofit. The records are admissible hearsay written statements if:

> The entries are made at or near the time of the event or act,
>
> A person with knowledge records the information or transmits the information to someone who records it,
>
> The records are kept in the course of a regularly conducted business activity or duty,
>
> The recording of the specific information is a regular practice of that business,
>
> The custodian or the qualified witness testifies to these facts, and
>
> The records are reliable and trustworthy.

The records witness must testify to the requirements of the business exception rule, which usually requires the examining attorney to ask leading questions to establish these requirements. In most civil cases and many criminal cases business records are introduced through a stipulation or in response to a request for an admission. There is usually no need to waste time to subpoena a witness to lay the foundation for the hearsay exception. Many of these records will also be self-authenticating under the rules of evidence and may be introduced through a witness who can testify to their relevance.

Example

In a commercial litigation case, Ms. Ecu testifies to the following:

> I am the manager of the business loan department, that it is the business of the bank to make and maintain records of loans, that Defendant's Exhibit No. 3 are loan documents made contemporaneously with the information recorded on the documents, and that the documents were made in the regular course of the business of the bank.

Exhibit No. 3 is admissible.

3.12 Public Records

Public records are reliable because government officials record the information pursuant to a public duty or the law and have no interest in recording information that favors one side or the other. Fed.R.Evid. 803(8). Several types of public records maintained by government agencies are admissible:

Records that describe or explain the activities of an office or agency, such as published reports by the government summarizing what the office or agency does. An example is a document published by a department of transportation which explains how it conducts drivers' licensing exams.

Records of matters observed and recorded pursuant to a duty imposed by law. Documents maintained by government officers concerning their official activities are examples of such records. Another example is public housing records listing the names of tenants and their addresses. Public reports containing observations of police officers or other law enforcement personnel are not generally permitted in criminal cases under this exception.

Factual findings resulting from investigations made pursuant to authority granted by law, such as reports prepared by government investigators. Only those parts of an investigation report that are factual findings, factual conclusions, and historical facts will be admissible. Conclusions or opinions are not admissible. For example, a fire investigative report which includes a description of the accident is admissible, but a portion of the report that concludes the fire was caused by arson because the defendant was in a desperate financial situation is inadmissible. In some cases, determining what is an admissible "factual finding" and what is an inadmissible "conclusion" is difficult. Courts have held that "factual conclusions" are admissible under the public records exception. The resolution in each case will depend upon the exact words contained in the report.

Land records and property documents maintained in a public office, including deeds, certificates, entries in ledgers, and computer data relating to property interests. These documents are reliable and admissible.

3.13 Other Specific Records

The rules of evidence in most jurisdictions render admissible the following specific types of documents:

Market reports and commercial data. Hearsay statements are contained in market reports, financial summaries, commercial documents, and business transaction data. These statements include facts, opinions, and evaluative or interpretive information. Examples are market quotations, stock prices, lists of financial information, business directories, and other compilations. The rationale for their admissibility is that since the financial and business world relies upon them, so should the law. (Fed.R.Evid. 803(17)).

Records of vital statistics, including birth, death, and marriage information. (Fed.R.Evid. 803(9)).

Records of religious organizations, including birth, marriage, divorce, death, and other personal or family records kept in the ordinary course of a religious organization's activities. (Fed.R.Evid. 803(11)).

Marriage, baptismal, and other certificates. (Fed.R.Evid. 803(12)).

Family records, including personal or family history or facts contained in Bibles, engravings, inscriptions, and other sources. (Fed.R.Evid. 803(13)).

Ancient documents and statements contained in authentic documents in existence for 20 years or more. (Fed.R.Evid. 803(16)).

Judgments of previous convictions and judgments involving personal, family, history, or boundary data. (Fed.R.Evid. 803(22) and (23)).

Many records are admissible under more than one hearsay exception. A record may qualify as a business record, public record, and a specific record. Some records may appear to be admissible under a rule but have been held to be inadmissible by the courts. For example, police reports are not admissible in criminal cases, even though such reports may technically qualify as business records or public records, because the defendant has a constitutional right to cross-examine witnesses, and a record cannot be cross-examined. Case decisions or statutes may expand or narrow the rules of evidence governing the introduction of various types of records.

3.14 Absence of Business or Public Records

The lack of an entry in a business or public record is admissible to prove an event did not occur. Fed.R.Evid. 803(7) and (10). Before the lack of a record or entry is admissible, the attorney must establish that the information was the type of information that would have been recorded and that a search has been made of the records. Most jurisdictions allow two ways to prove there was a search and there are no records. A witness with personal knowledge may testify to the search that was undertaken, or the proponent may offer a self-authenticating certificate which describes the diligent but unsuccessful search.

3.15 Past Recollection Recorded

Records concerning a matter that a witness no longer remembers, but that the witness once knew and accurately recorded when the matter was fresh, will be admissible evidence. Fed.R.Evid. 803(5). Written records of prior events are admissible if:

> The testifying witness does not presently fully or accurately recall the event,
>
> The witness has personal knowledge of the record,

The witness made the record or adopted it as correct at a time when the memory of the witness was fresh, usually close in time to the occurrence of the event, and

The witness testifies that the report is accurate, or testifies that the record would not have been signed or adopted if it were inaccurate.

Section 6.45 describes the introduction of a past recollection recorded document.

Example

In an antitrust case, the witness maintained a telephone log of phone conversations made three years before the trial which summarizes a particular telephone conversation. At trial, the witness will not be able to remember the details of a three-year-old telephone conversation. The telephone log may be admitted as past recollection recorded by having the witness establish the existence of the four foundation factors for past recollection recorded.

3.16 Learned Treatises

A learned treatise is a book, periodical, article, pamphlet, or magazine established as reliable authority on a matter, ordinarily the subject of expert opinion, which is relied upon by an expert in direct examination or called to the attention of an expert witness during cross-examination. Fed.R.Evid. 803(10).

3.17 Reputation Evidence

Reputation evidence is a collection of hearsay statements in which specific hearsay exceptions render certain types of relevant reputation evidence admissible. Reputation evidence concerning personal or family history, such as marriages, births, deaths or other events of family significance are admissible. Fed.R.Evid. 803(19). Reputation evidence regarding general history or land boundaries or customs is also admissible. Fed.R.Evid. 803(20). Reputation evidence of a person's character among associates or in the community is likewise admissible as a hearsay exception. Fed.R.Evid. 803(21).

3.18 Declarant Unavailable

Some hearsay statements are only admissible if the declarant is unavailable to testify. Fed.R.Evid. 804(a). The "unavailability" of a witness includes situations in which the declarant:

- Is absent from the hearing and the proponent of the statement is unable to procure attendance through a subpoena or other process.
- Is unable to be present because of an existing physical or mental illness or death.
- Testifies to a lack of memory of the subject matter of the statement.
- Is exempted from testifying by a court ruling on the ground of privilege.
- Persists in refusing to testify despite a court order.

Hearsay statements that are admissible if the declarant is unavailable include:

Former testimony,

Statements against interest,

Statements of personal or family history, and

Dying declarations.

3.19 Former Testimony

The testimony given by a witness at a deposition or another hearing may be admitted if the party against whom the testimony is offered had an opportunity to previously examine the witness. Fed.R.Evid. 804(b)(1). The most common use of former testimony involves the introduction of deposition testimony because the lay or expert witness is unavailable. In criminal cases, this hearsay exception is less often applicable because of the defendant's constitutional right to cross-examine witnesses during the trial.

3.20 Statements Against Interest

A statement made by a person contrary to that person's interests is admissible. Fed.R.Evid. 803(b)(3). The contrary interests include statements adversely affecting a person's pecuniary or proprietary interests or which tend to subject the person to civil or criminal liability. The rationale for this rule is that reasonable individuals do not make statements against their own interests unless those statements are accurate. This exception need only be used where the declarant is not a party. If a party makes such a statement, the statement is admissible as a party admission.

Example

In a civil arson case, the owner of the building has been denied coverage and has sued the insurance company. An employee of a non-party of the building made a statement to the fire marshal. The plaintiff calls the fire marshal to testify.

Examining Attorney:

Q: What happened to Mr. Marlboro?

A.   He died in a horse riding accident.

Q: What did Mr. Marlboro tell you when you investigated the fire?

Objecting Lawyer:

Objection. Hearsay.

Judge:

Overruled.

A: Mr. Marlboro told me that he and others routinely smoked in the service garage in violation of company policy.

3.21 Statements of Personal or Family History

Statements regarding the personal or family history of the declarant are admissible. Fed.R.Evid. 803(b)(4). These statements are generally allowed as long as the declarant was related to a person or intimately involved in a family and likely to have accurate information even though the declarant had no means of personally knowing the matter.

Example

In a probate case, a daughter is called to testify to what her father had told her.

Examining Attorney:

    Q: What did your father tell you about his family?

Objecting Lawyer:

        Objection. Hearsay.

Judge:

        Overruled.

    A: My father told me he had one brother who had nine heads and that his name was Hydra.

3.22 Dying Declaration

A statement concerning the cause or circumstance of the declarant's impending death which is made by the declarant who believes death is imminent is admissible. Fed.R.Evid. 803(b)(2). The rationale is that the declarant, who faces death, is telling the truth. If the declarant doesn't die, the exception is not available.

Example

In a murder case, the victim's husband is called to testify by the prosecution.

Examining Attorney:

    Q: After your wife was shot, what did you do?

    A: I ran over and knelt next to her.

    Q: What did she say?

Objecting Lawyer:

        Objection. Hearsay.

Judge:

> Overruled.

A: She said, "I'm not going to make it." And then she told me, "The butler did it."

3.23 Residual Hearsay Exception

Hearsay statements that are not covered by a specific hearsay exception may be admissible if:

The statement is offered as evidence of a material fact;

No other evidence exists which is more probative;

Its admission will serve the interests of justice; and

The offering party provides opposing counsel with prior notice of the introduction of such a statement.

This "residual" or "catch-all" exception to the hearsay rule may render other reliable, trustworthy hearsay admissible. (Fed.R.Evid. 803(24) and 804(5). This exception is useful in limited situations where no other rule or exception permits reliable and trustworthy hearsay to be admissible. This exception is not intended to and has not been interpreted by courts to make inadmissible hearsay admissible. The exception is reserved for unusual circumstances in which a reliable and trustworthy hearsay statement should be admissible in the interests of justice because no other exception covers the situation. For example, hearsay statements made by consumers who report their experiences with a product in a consumer survey may be deemed to be admissible under this residual exception.

3.24 Multiple Hearsay

A statement may contain more than one hearsay statement. This multiple form of hearsay is called "hearsay within hearsay." Fed.R.Evid. 805. Each statement must be analyzed to determine whether there is multiple hearsay and whether each part of the statement fall within an exception or are defined as non-hearsay.

A common situation of multiple hearsay occurs with documents. Most documents introduced during trial contain hearsay information. The document may contain admissible statements and inadmissible hearsay. Each document must be analyzed to determine which sentences, phrases, and words are admissible and which are not. Inadmissible information should be deleted.

Example of Testimony

Curley sues Moe for civil assault. At trial, Curley testifies that "Moe said to me, I meant to poke you in the eyes because Larry said he was in a lot of pain because you had just slapped him." The attorney for Moe objects to this multiple hearsay. There are two statements within this testimony: the statement by Moe to Curley and the statement by Larry to Curley. The first statement—that of Moe to Curley—is a party admission and is admissible. The second statement—that of Larry to Curley—is admissible as a hearsay exception, either as a present sense impression or as a statement of an existing physical condition. The entire statement is admissible.

Example of Document

A plaintiff lays a foundation through a medical record custodian that a hospital record falls within a business record exception to the hearsay rule.

The witness is a medical doctor, Dr. Blue. The exhibit is the plaintiff's medical record offered by the plaintiff. The witness testifies that she is the Director of the Hospital Emergency Room, that it is the business of the hospital to make such medical records, that this exhibit was made contemporaneously with the events recorded, and that the record was made in the regular course of the business of the emergency room.

The record falls within the business record exception to the hearsay rule. Parts of the record may be admissible or inadmissible depending upon the application of hearsay exceptions. The record contains the following statements:

A Statement By Dr. Blue: "Administered antibiotics to the patient." Admissible. Business record exception.

A Statement By Dr. Mauve: "Set patient's broken arm in a cast." Admissible. Business record exception.

A Statement By the Plaintiff: "My head hurts." Admissible. Statement by person made for purposes of diagnosis.

A Statement By the Defendant: "I was driving around 30 m.p.h. when I hit the rear end of her car." Admissible. Party admission offered against that party.

A Statement By a Bystander in the Emergency Room: "Wow, her (referring to the plaintiff) head was all covered with blood right after the accident." Admissible, by most judges. Present sense impression.

A Statement By a Witness to the Accident: "He (referring to the defendant) sure looked drunk to me when I saw him later after the accident." Inadmissible, by most courts. No exception applies.

C. FINAL ANALYSIS

3.25 Questionable Objections

Certain objections—some of which are commonly made—are improper, inapplicable, inappropriate, or not recognized in a jurisdiction. These improper objections vary among jurisdictions, and include the following:

Irrelevant, Immaterial, Incompetent.
This broad objection may be inappropriate because it is too general. Irrelevancy is a proper ground for an objection. "Immaterial" is no longer a term recognized by the Federal Rules of Evidence. "Incompetent" refers to the ability of a witness to testify and not to specific questions or answers.

Improper and Unfair.
This objection is too general and does not specify the ground of an objection. A reference to a more specific reason must be made, or this objection will usually be overruled.

Self-Serving.

This objection is usually groundless. In a general sense, every item of evidence the opposing side attempts to introduce is self-serving, that is, it will serve that side's best interests and harm the other side's case.

Prejudicial.

This objection is also improper, for reasons similar to the inappropriateness of the self-serving objection. It is not sufficient that evidence is prejudicial for it to be excluded, the evidence has to be "unfairly prejudicial." See Fed.R.Evid. 403.

Invades the Province of the Fact Finder.

This objection may be too ambiguous to be useful. An expert witness can testify to an ultimate opinion; lay witnesses are able to testify to many common opinions. These admissible responses can be said to invade the province of the fact finder.

Begging.

This is not really an objection, but a plea for mercy. The attorney should approach the bench with shoulders drooped and a vacant look. Nothing need be said. The judge may help if the judge had a similar experience as an attorney.

3.26 Summary Objections—Improper Form of Question

Leading

FRE 611

Lawyer Testifying

Narrative

FRE 611

No Question Before Witness

Non-Responsive

FRE 611

Volunteered

Cumulative/Repetitious

FRE 403 & 611

Asked and Answered

Vague

FRE 401–403

Ambiguous
Confusing
Misleading
Unintelligible

Multiple Questions

FRE 611

Compound Questions

Assuming Facts Not in Evidence

FRE 611 & 701–704

Inaccurate
Hypothetical

Misstatement of Testimony

FRE 611

Mischaracterization of Evidence

Argumentative

FRE 611

Badgering

Improper Impeachment

FRE 613

Collateral Issue

Beyond Scope

FRE 613

3.27　Summary Objections—Exclusionary Rules of Evidence

Relevancy

>FRE 401–411
>>Irrelevant
>>No Probative Value
>>Unfairly Prejudicial
>>>Improper Character
>>>Improper Habit
>>>Subsequent Remedial Measures
>>>Offers of Compromise
>>>Payment of Medical Expenses
>>>Plea Bargains
>>>Liability Insurance
>>>Religious Beliefs/Opinions

Privileges

>FRE 501
>>Attorney/Client
>>Doctor/Patient
>>Spousal Testimony
>>Marital Communications
>>Clergy/Penitent
>>Trade/Business Secrets
>>Informer Identity
>>Governmental Information
>>News Sources
>>Other

Competence

>FRE 601–602
>>Incompetent
>>Lack of Personal Knowledge
>>Lack of Memory

Foundation

FRE 601–602
> Lack of Foundation

Lay Opinion

FRE 701
> Impermissible Opinion
> Impermissible Conclusion
> Speculation

Expert Opinion

FRE 702–705
> Unqualified Witness
> Impermissible Opinion

Authentication

FRE 901–902
> Lack of Authenticity

Original Writings

FRE 1001–1007
> Signs
> Independent Facts
> Collateral Matter
> Unauthentic Copy
> Non-genuine Original

Parol Evidence

> Statutory or Case Law

Criminal Constitutional Issues

3.28 Summary Objections—Hearsay Analysis

Hearsay

> Declarant
>> Not Under Oath
>> Not Subject to Cross
>> Credibility Not Observable

Definition

> FRE 801
>> Offered to Prove Truth of Statement?
>> Out-of-Court Statement?
>> Assertive or Nonassertive?
>> Non-propositions
>> Verbal Acts
>> Declarant Not Person

Non-hearsay

> FRE 801(d)
>> Party Admissions
>> Prior Statements

Hearsay Exceptions

> Sense Impressions
>> Present Sense Impression 803(1)
>> Excited Utterance 803(2)
> State of Mind
>> Existing Mental/Emotional/Physical Condition 803(3)
>> Treatment Medical Statements 803(4)
> Records/Documents/Writings
>> Business Records 803(6)
>> Public Records 803(8)
>> Past Recollection Recorded 803(5)
>> Vital Statistics 803(9)
>> Absent Entries 803(7) & (10)
>> Commercial Data 803(17)
>> Property Records 803(14) & (15)

Official Certificates 803(11) & (12)
Family Records 803(13)
Ancient Documents 803(16)
Learned Treatises 803(18)
Previous Convictions 803(22)
Other Judgments 803(23)

Reputation
Character 803(21)
Family 803(19)
General History 803(26)

Declarant Not Available
Former Testimony 804(b)(1)
Statement Against Interest 804(b)(3)
Personal History 804(b)(4)
Dying Declaration 804(b)(2)

Reliable Hearsay 803(25) & 804(b)(5)

RESOURCES

Bibliography

The Catchall Exceptions to the Hearsay Rule: Merging Rules 803(24) and 804(b)(5) of the Federal Rules of Evidence, Kathryn J. Stumpf, 37 *Federation of Insurance & Corporate Counsel Quarterly* 73–96 (1986).

Challenges and Objections Need Intelligent Preparation, Bruce A. Friedman and Reynolds T. Cafferate, 106 *The Los Angeles Daily J.* 7 (1993).

Error Preservation in Civil Litigation: A Primer for the Iowa Practitioner, Robert G. Albee and Kasey W. Kincaid, 35 *Drake L. R.* 1–26 (1986).

I Object! An Expert's List of Basic Trial Objections, James W. McElhaney, 78 *ABA J.* 90 (1992).

Making and Meeting Objections, Forest W. Hanna, 57 *UMKC L. R.* 809–820 (1989).

Making and Meeting Objections, Howard P. Sweeney, 27 *Air Force L. R.* 171–180 (1987).

Objecting (to courtroom evidence), Steven Lubet, 16 *American J. of Trial Advocacy* 213–253 (1992).

Objections at Trial, Myron H. Bright, Ronald L. Carlson (Butterworth Legal Publishers 1990).

The Supreme Court and the Interpretation of the Federal Rules of Evidence, Glen Weissenberger, 53 *Ohio State L. J.* 1307–1339 (1992).

Think Before You Object: Knowing When to Speak and When to Keep Quiet is an Art, Harry P. Hall and Stuart W. Snow, 6 *Family Advocate* 4–6 (1983).

Trial Objections, Mark A. Dombroff (Ford Pub. 1985–).

Trial Objections (Examining Witnesses), John C. Conti, 14 *Litigation* 16 (1987).

Trial Objections Handbook, Roger C. Park (Shepard's/McGraw-Hill 1991).

The Trial of Celebrated Criminal Cases: An Analysis of Evidentiary Objections, John W. Poulos, 56 *Tulane L. R.* 602 (1982).

When to Object, James W. McElhaney, 74 *ABA J.* 98 June (1989).

Video

Basic Concepts in Evidence, National Institute For Trial Advocacy (1975).

Evidentiary Objections, National Institute For Trial Advocacy (1979).

Failure of Recollection, Best Evidence Rule, Perception, National Institute For Trial Advocacy (1975).

Hearsay I, National Institute For Trial Advocacy (1975).

Hearsay II, National Institute For Trial Advocacy (1975).

Hearsay III, National Institute For Trial Advocacy (1975).

Hearsay IV, National Institute For Trial Advocacy (1975).

Introduction to Evidence, National Institute For Trial Advocacy (1975).

The Ten Commandments of Cross Examination, National Institute For Trial Advocacy (1975).

Trial Evidence—Making and Meeting Objections, National Institute For Trial Advocacy (1991).

Film

Body of Evidence (1993).

Secret Evidence (1941).

CHAPTER 4
EXHIBITS

Art, whose honesty must work through artifice,
cannot avoid cheating truth.

— Laura Riding
Selected Poems in Five Sets

A. SCOPE

4.01 Types of Exhibits

People watch the evening news, Sesame Street, The Wheel of Fortune, MTV, *Gone With the Wind*, *Lawrence of Arabia*, and *Who Framed Roger Rabbit*. They read newspapers and magazines filled with dramatic, interesting color photos and graphics. People seldom sit around and listen to the spoken word. It takes more than talk to keep people interested. It takes visual aids to help people learn and remember. This is just as true in legal proceedings as it is anywhere else.

Well-prepared and well-presented exhibits help the witnesses and the advocates communicate much more effectively and present an interesting and persuasive case. There are three major types of exhibits: real evidence, demonstrative evidence, and visual aids. Some commentators use different terms to explain these categories of exhibits, but everyone recognizes their existence and use.

4.01.1 Real Evidence

Real evidence consists of exhibits which are objects or writings that are facts in a case. Real evidence includes physical objects and documentary writings, such as the gun used in a homicide, the chainsaw involved in a product liability case, and the written contract in a contract case. These tangible items of real evidence are probative in and by themselves. Real evidence is admitted into evidence as part of the record, and is available to the fact finder to use in deliberation.

Sample Dialogue

Q: I have just handed you an exhibit which has been marked for identification as Plaintiff's Exhibit No. 2. Do you recognize Plaintiff's Exhibit No. 2?

A: Yes.

Q: How do you recognize Plaintiff's Exhibit No. 2?

A: I recognize it by its title and by my initials which I wrote on it right after I took it from the defendant's hands.

Q: What is Plaintiff's Exhibit No. 2?

A: It's the book entitled *Ghandi* that I saw the defendant use to hit the plaintiff in the face.

Q: Is Plaintiff's Exhibit No. 2 in the same condition as it was when you saw the defendant hit the plaintiff in the face?

A: Yes.

To the Court:

Your Honor, at this time I offer Plaintiff's Exhibit No. 2 in evidence.

Real evidence adds another dimension of proof. A physical object or document provides the fact finder with a lasting impression of certain trustworthy facts. For example, the claw hammer murder weapon can be seen; the defective lantern can be touched; the signature on the lengthy, small-print contract can be viewed; the written libelous statement can be seen; the bar admission certification can be admired.

4.01.2 Demonstrative Evidence

Demonstrative evidence refers to those exhibits which are not a part of the "real" event of the case. These exhibits are usually created after the event and have no intrinsic probative value. Demonstrative or illustrative evidence includes diagrams, charts, graphs, models, movable figures, computer graphics, videotapes, and anything else that augments verbal testimony. These exhibits are admissible if they:

> Assist a witness in testifying, or
>
> Help the fact finder understand the evidence.

Photographs may be taken and used in a variety of cases for a variety of purposes. In automobile accident cases, photographs of the scene, the automobiles, and injuries to the injured parties are common. A videotape of the day in the life of a severely injured and handicapped plaintiff may be made and shown. Photographs of the scene of the crime are typical in criminal cases. Aerial photographs may be used in condemnation proceedings. Slides, a movie or a videotape of a testing procedure or of a demonstration may be made and shown.

Photographs are usually demonstrative evidence. Some photographs constitute real evidence. A film of a bank robbery taken with a surveillance camera, a photograph of a physical injury, an aerial photograph of land boundaries, may be actual evidence of facts in a case. The foundation for real or demonstrative photographs is usually the same. The witness' testimony that the photograph, slide, movie, computer graphic or videotape accurately depicts what appears is sufficient to establish foundation. In some cases, a witness may have to testify as to how the photograph, movie or videotape was made, if the making affects the authenticity or accuracy of the reproduction.

A witness may use a prepared diagram or may create a freehand drawing on a blackboard, whiteboard, or easel paper using marking pens. While freehand drawings may have to be used because of time or financial constraints, prepared diagrams are much more effective because few witnesses draw well extemporaneously. Enlargements of simple prepared diagrams can be made inexpensively and quickly.

Diagrams and drawings need not be drawn to exact scale, but neither can they be distorted depictions. Demonstrative evidence need not be exact, but must not inaccurately portray the facts. The same restrictions apply to other types of demonstrative evidence such as models, charts, and graphic displays.

Sample Dialogue

Q: You have in your hands what is marked for identification as Defendant's Exhibit F. Do you recognize it?

A: Yes.

Q: What is Defendant's Exhibit F?

A: It is a diagram of the classroom.

Q: Is the diagram a fair and accurate diagram of the law school classroom that you saw and sat in for two years?

A: Yes.

Q: Would this diagram assist you in explaining what you saw when you were awakened?

A: Yes, it would.

To the Court:

Your Honor, at this time I offer Defendant's Exhibit F as illustrative evidence, and ask that the witness be allowed to use it during her testimony.

Demonstrative evidence adds a powerful visual dimension to the trial. The fact finder can be significantly influenced by the use of illustrative exhibits. A prepared diagram can provide an overview of an event; a photograph can bring to life the details of a scene; a videotape can show the lengthy, deliberate path the defendant took going to the murder scene to establish premedition; a working model with movable figures can demonstrate a product; a metal diagram of an intersection with magnetic cars can assist a witness in telling the story of an accident. Computer technology has provided new opportunities to create charts, graphs and other visual aids. This technology also permits the creation of simulations and recreations that can be very persuasive, but also very expensive.

4.01.3 Visual Aids

V isual aids are created and used by advocates to effectively communicate information to the fact finder and to help the fact finder understand the presentation. Visual aids are neither real nor demonstrative exhibits and are not considered evidence. Visual aids may be used during final argument, opening statement, and direct and cross-examination. Examples of visual aids include: a prepared chart summarizing evidence; overhead transparencies summarizing expert testimony; a part of opening statement prepared for an overhead projector; a blown-up verdict form to be used during final argument; and a whiteboard, flip chart, or easel paper written on by the attorney listing words, dates, amounts, or other testimony of a witness during direct or cross-examination.

Visual aids can persuasively emphasize evidence and arguments. A line or bar graph can be designed that favorably portrays evidence. Summaries of testimony can highlight evidence. Prepared lists of words and phrases placed on taped or velcro-backed strips can be placed on a chart creating an outline of an argument. The advocate's resume can be displayed to whoever has the patience to read it.

Visual aids are often not marked as exhibits and are not received in evidence. Although there is no specific foundation that ordinarily must be established to use visual aids, it is usually necessary to either advise the judge of their intended use or to obtain permission.

B. PREPARING EXHIBITS

Exhibits can have a great impact on the fact finder. The process for planning and using exhibits includes several preliminary considerations:

> The identification of potential exhibits.
>
> Assessing the use of exhibits.
>
> Planning a professional presentation.
>
> Selecting the witness.
>
> Managing exhibits.

4.02 Identifying Potential Exhibits

The identification of exhibits occurs during the fact investigation before the proceeding. This is when real evidence, is located, gathered, and preserved. Real evidence, consisting of physical objects and documentary writings, which are potential exhibits include objects such as weapons, clothing, products, appliances, x-rays, test results, laboratory analyses, and documents such as letters, memos, correspondence, contracts, leases, bills, checks, business records, computer data, and other writings and recordings.

Demonstrative evidence is obtained or created prior to and during the proceeding. The preparation of potential illustrative exhibits includes the taking of photographs, including prints and slides, the making of movies and audio/videotape recordings, the design of diagrams such as charts and graphs, computer graphics, and the creation of exhibit summaries. As the date for the proceeding approaches and final preparations are made for opening and closing statements and witness examinations, proposed visual aids are reviewed, selected, and designed for use.

4.03 Assessing the Use of Exhibits

Advocates select exhibits that effectively communicate the case theory, present substantive information to the fact finder, emphasize important areas of evidence, refute the opponent's evidence, and persuade the fact finder of the truth of what happened. The following questions are factors that should be considered in the use of an exhibit:

Will the exhibit enhance the ability of the witness to testify more effectively? If the exhibit will assist a witness in describing or explaining testimony, it should be used. Part of the direct examination preparation involves the attorney rehearsing the introduction and use of the exhibit with the witness.

Will the fact finder better understand and remember the evidence portrayed by the exhibit? If the exhibit distracts or confuses the fact finder, it should be not be used.

Can the foundation for the exhibit be established through the testifying witness? Some exhibits involve a "chain of custody" foundation, and may require more than one witness to testify before an exhibit is introduced or used.

Will the exhibit take too long to introduce or use? The advocate should efficiently introduce and use the exhibit.

Does the relevant, probative value of the exhibit outweigh any unfair prejudicial impact? If the exhibit shocks the fact finder, is vulgar or in bad taste, or is unnecessarily cumulative or repetitive, it should not be offered.

What is the cost and amount of time needed to make or obtain the exhibit? The expense, in dollars and time, should not exceed the exhibit's overall usefulness. The decision to use an exhibit must be made far enough in advance so the exhibit may be prepared or obtained before the case.

Will the exhibit be perceived by the fact finder as unfair? Expensive or numerous exhibits used by one side and not employed by the other side may cause the fact finder to perceive the case of a party with significant resources overwhelming a party of lesser resources.

What technical problems might there be with the exhibit? Is the exhibit too big or too small? Have adequate steps been taken to ensure these problems can be overcome?

Is the exhibit color coordinated with the advocate's clothes?

4.04 Planning a Professional Presentation

The advocate must be able to introduce and use exhibits in a professional manner. Advance preparation is needed for most exhibits. The advocate should prepare and rehearse ahead of time so that exhibits are marked appropriately; the introduction and use of the exhibit is coordinated; charts are flipped at the right time; the model functions; the overhead projector is plugged in and is working; the computer graphic can be accessed easily; and everything goes smoothly. An advocate needs to determine what equipment—such as a blackboard, whiteboard, easel pad, projector screen, x-ray imaging box—will be available. Other items that might be needed include: video monitors, video playback machines (VCR's), slide projectors, computers, and extension cords.

Exhibits that are introduced into evidence and used in a professional manner will have a positive impact on the fact finder. Careful use of movement, stance, and positioning can increase the impact that an exhibit has, but awkward positioning and obstructing the fact finder's view may diminish the exhibit's effectiveness.

4.05 Selecting the Witness

Exhibits are often introduced through a witness. This procedure requires that a witness or witnesses be selected who are qualified to identify and lay a foundation for the admission of an exhibit. The advocate must prepare the witness in advance so the witness can answer the qualification and foundation questions and is comfortable with the exhibit and the courtroom.

4.06 Managing Exhibits

Organization is of particular importance in introducing and using exhibits. Specific reference sheets itemizing the exhibits to be used, the necessary foundation for those exhibits, and the witnesses who will provide that necessary foundation are helpful. This organized format assists in preparing for the exhibit's admission into evidence and provides a quick reference as to which exhibits have been or need to be offered into evidence.

4.07 Introducing and Using Exhibits

The introduction and use of exhibits involves a number of considerations:

> Reviewing evidentiary issues and problems.
>
> Understanding the procedures applicable to the introduction and use of exhibits.
>
> Determining the precise questions needed for the foundation and use of the exhibits.
>
> Anticipating objections to the trial exhibits.

The remainder of this chapter explains these considerations in detail.

C. EVIDENTIARY ISSUES

Real and demonstrative exhibits are subject to the rules of evidence like any other item of evidence. The judge has discretion to admit or not admit specific evidence. Some exhibits, like physical objects, may be easy to introduce. Other exhibits, such as documentary evidence, have to satisfy evidence rules regarding the admissibility of hearsay and original writings before being received into evidence. Possible objections to exhibits must be considered in developing proper foundation for the exhibit's admissibility. This section discusses additional concerns applicable to exhibits including:

> Relevancy and unfair prejudice.
>
> The foundation needed to establish admissibility and persuasiveness.
>
> A chain of custody.
>
> Exhibits used for limited purposes.
>
> The redaction of an exhibit.
>
> The exercise of judicial discretion.

4.08 Is it Relevant or Unfairly Prejudicial?

An exhibit must be relevant to be admissible. An exhibit is relevant if it has any tendency to make more or less probable the existence of any fact that is of consequence to the determination of the action.

Sample Dialogue

In a personal injury matter resulting from a car accident assume the witness has testified during the morning and the testimony continues after lunch.

Direct Examiner:

Q: I am showing you what has been marked for identification as Plaintiff's Exhibit No. 10. Do you recognize it, Mr. Dumbo?

A: Yes.

Q: How?

A: I brought it with me from lunch.

Q: What is it?

A: It is a peanut shell. I ate the peanut part for lunch.

Q: Why did you have peanuts for lunch?

A: They help my memory so I can testify later.

To the Judge:

    I offer Plaintiff's Exhibit No. 10.

Opposing Advocate:

    I object to this exhibit. It has nothing to do with this matter and is irrelevant.

Judge:

    Objection sustained.

Even when an exhibit is relevant, it may be excluded from evidence if it tends to confuse the issues or mislead the fact finder, distorts the facts, causes undue delay, wastes time, is needless and cumulative, or if the probative value of the exhibit is substantially outweighed by its unfair prejudicial impact. The attorney should consider bringing a motion in limine and presenting any potentially prejudicial or gruesome exhibits prior to the case to seek a ruling regarding their admissibility.

Some exhibits may be susceptible to a claim of prejudice because of their visual impact. This impact may indeed be prejudicial to the opponent, but such harm is not necessarily unfair. For example, a photograph showing injuries that a plaintiff has suffered demonstrates the extent of the injury and communicates the pain and suffering the plaintiff endured. The impact of this photograph is undoubtedly more harmful to the defendant's case than if the plaintiff orally described the injuries. This harm does not rise to the level of unfair prejudice as defined by the rules of evidence unless the exhibit is unnecessarily gruesome.

Example (Criminal Case)

Assume the prosecution is introducing a series of photographs of the deceased victim through a police officer.

Examining Attorney:

Q: Officer Furillo, I am showing you what has been marked for identification as State's Exhibit No. 84. It is a photograph. Do you recognize this photograph?

A: Yes, I do.

Q: What is it?

A: It is another photograph in the series you have just shown me of the body of the victim.

Q: Is it also, like the other five photographs I have shown you, a fair and accurate representation of the victim's body as you saw it on the day of the murder?

A: Yes, it is.

To the Court:

Your Honor, I offer State's Exhibit No. 84.

Opposing Counsel:

Your Honor, I object to the introduction of Exhibit No. 84 on the grounds that it is unduly prejudicial, a waste of time, needless and cumulative.

Judge:

Your objection is sustained.

Example (Civil Case)

Assume the witness is an eyewitness to an auto accident that occurred at 9 p.m. on a summer night.

Examining Attorney:

Q: Ms. Avalon, I show you what is marked for identification as Defendant's Exhibit C. Do you recognize this photograph?

A: Yes.

Q: What does it show?

A: It shows the intersection where the accident happened.

Q: Is Defendant's Exhibit C a fair and accurate representation of the scene of the intersection that you saw?

A: Yes, for the most part.

To the Court:

Your Honor, I offer Defendant's Exhibit C into evidence.

Opposing Counsel:

> I object, your Honor, to the introduction of Defendant's Exhibit C. This photograph was taken during the day and does not show the intersection as the witness saw it at dusk, after the sun had set. The photograph distorts the evidence and is likely to confuse and mislead the jury.

Judge:

> Sustained.

4.09 Levels of Foundation

There are two levels of foundation for exhibits. The first is the evidentiary foundation which must be established before the exhibit can be admitted as evidence, and the second is the persuasive foundation. The judge or arbitrator always determines whether the evidentiary foundation has been met and whether the exhibit is admitted in evidence. The fact finder, different, determines the persuasive weight and whether the exhibit is believable.

The advocate must meet the evidentiary foundation requirement in order to have an exhibit received into evidence. This threshold foundation is the absolute minimum requirement for the admissibility of an exhibit. While the admissibility foundation for the introduction of an exhibit may be quite easy to meet, the attorney must expand, simplify, or clarify the foundation to increase the weight the fact finder will give to that exhibit. This persuasive foundation is testimony that enhances the credibility and weight of an exhibit and is as important as the admissibility foundation.

4.09.1 Evidentiary Foundation

The foundation for real evidence is established by a witness testifying that the tangible object or document is what it is claimed to be. Federal Rule of Evidence 901(b)(1). The nature and extent of the admissibility foundation depends upon the type of real evidence being admitted. There are two primary types of real evidence:

> Real evidence that is readily identifiable because it is unique or singular, and

> Real evidence that is fungible and which lacks unique or readily identifiable characteristics.

The minimum evidentiary foundation is established for a piece of real evidence when a witness can identify the object by its distinctive characteristics and can state that the object is in substantially the same condition as it was at a relevant time. Federal Rule of Evidence 901(b)(4) permits identification by "distinctive characteristics" such as "appearance, contents, substance, internal patterns, or other distinctive characteristics . . . ."

Sample Dialogue

Direct Examiner:

Q: I show you what is marked for identification as Defendant's Exhibit No. 1. What is it?

A: It is my rubber duckie.

Q: How do you recognize it?

A: It looks identical to my rubber duckie. It is the same shape and color. It feels the same. And it has the same water marks on it from the last time I used it.

Q: Is Defendant's Exhibit No. 1 in the same, or substantially the same, condition now as it was when you last saw it in your bathtub?

A: Yes.

To the Judge:

> I offer Defendant's Exhibit No. 1, a rubber duckie, into evidence.

Evidence law does not require that a witness be completely sure or state with absolute certainty that an exhibit is the identical object. An exhibit will be admitted with qualified testimony as long as there is reasonable evidence to support a finding that the exhibit is what it is claimed to be. A qualified identification of an exhibit may affect the weight the fact finder gives to the exhibit but does not affect admissibility.

4.09.2　Persuasive Foundation

After sufficient evidence has been established to admit an exhibit, additional testimony may be needed to convince a fact finder that the exhibit is real, accurate, complete, or true. The extent of this persuasive foundation evidence depends upon the type of exhibit introduced. The following example illustrates the levels of evidentiary foundation and persuasive foundation with respect to the opinion testimony of an expert regarding an exhibit. The more facts that are admitted regarding the authenticity or accuracy of an exhibit, the more likely that the fact finder will conclude the exhibit is what it is claimed to be.

Sample Dialogue

Assume Sherlock Holmes has been qualified as an expert crime laboratory analyst and has analyzed two separate bullets: one from the body of the deceased and the other from the test gun.

Direct Examiner:

Q:　You have told us that you examined what has been marked for identification as state's Exhibit A—a bullet from the body of the deceased?

A:　Yes.

Q:　Did you examine state's Exhibit B, which is the bullet you told us was fired from the test gun?

A:　Indeed.

Q:　Did you compare them?

A:　Of course.

Q:　How did you do that?

A:　With a comparison microscope.

Q: What is a comparison microscope?

A: A comparison microscope is an instrument which allows me to put two bullets under separate eyepieces so they can be rotated, and I can look for similarities in both the vertical and horizontal markings on the bullets.

Q: Based on your examination with the comparison microscope, do you have an opinion whether the bullet from the body of the deceased matches the bullet fired from the test gun?

A: I do.

Q: What is it?

A: They match identically.

Q: Describe to us how you made this comparison.

A: The markings on both bullets, which are known as striations, matched.

Q: What caused the striations?

A: Originally, a singing group from MoTown I believe.

Q: I meant in this case.

A: Sorry, ol' chap. Striations are caused by scratches and imperfections in the barrel of the pistol which causes marks or striations on the bullet.

Q: How do these striations help you make bullet comparisons?

A: These striation markings will be the same on every bullet fired from the same gun.

Q: Do you have an opinion whether the bullets, Exhibits A and B, were fired from the same gun?

A: Yes.

Q: What is the opinion?

A: They were fired from the same gun.

Q: How do you know?

A: It was quite elementary. I rotated the bullets so I could see the scratches or striations on the bullets were identical.

4.10 Establishing a Chain of Custody

The foundation for most exhibits can be established through a witness who testifies that an exhibit looks or feels like the real thing. Some exhibits, particularly physical objects, may not be identifiable through the senses of a witness. Objects that are not unique, that do not have distinctive characteristics, or that have not been marked in any identifiable way, may require a "chain of custody" foundation to make the exhibit admissible. A chain of custody accounts for the whereabouts of the exhibit during all relevant times of the case. For example, in a drug case, the plastic bag containing the drug may need to be accounted for from the time the bag was seized from the defendant until its transportation to the courtroom. For another example, in a contaminated beverage case, the glass bottle needs to be accounted for from the time of consumption until the proceeding.

There are two primary ways of establishing an unbroken chain of custody:

> The exhibit at all times has been in the safe, continuing, and sole possession of one or more individuals; or

> The exhibit itself was distinctively identified, or was sealed and placed in a safe, tamper-proof container.

Testimony from one or more witnesses must show there have been no significant breaks in the links of the chain of custody. Typically, evidence need not establish an unbroken chain or the whereabouts of an exhibit over the entire period of relevant time. The chain of custody is flexible, and qualified evidence is sufficient to meet the admissibility foundation. Additional evidence may be necessary to meet the persuasive foundation and convince the fact finder that the exhibit is the actual real evidence and there has been no loss, misplacement, mix-up, unexplained changes, or tampering.

Sample Dialogue

This example illustrates how the chain of custody is established when the exhibit has been in the continual, sole possession of individuals.

Direct Examiner (*First Witness*):

Q: On May 2, at 12:00 noon, where were you?

A: I was at the Mudville Ball Park.

Q: What were you doing there?

A: I was there with my wife and my son, and we were having a picnic before the team began batting practice for the big game.

Q: What happened?

A: One of the baseball players came out to home plate before anyone else even arrived.

Q: Did you know who it was?

A: Yes.

Q: Who?

A: Casey.

Q: How do you know it was him?

A: I recognized him. I had seen him many times before at games and in town.

Q: What did he do?

A: I'm not sure. I wasn't paying attention.

Q: What happened?

A: I heard the sound of a crack of a bat.

Q: Then what?

A: Well, I was quite surprised.

Q: Why?

A: Because it was long before any batting practice or the game.

Q: What happened next?

A: I was suddenly hit on the head by a ball.

Q: What happened to you?

A: I ended up with a big cut on my head.

Q: What did you do?

A: I picked up the ball.

Q: Then what did you do with it?

A: I gave it to my son.

Q: Did you look at it carefully?

A: No, I was bleeding a lot.

Q: Can you identify the baseball that hit you on the head?

A: No.

Q: Why not?

A: I wouldn't recognize it.

Q: Why?

A: Because it looked like any other baseball.

Direct Examiner (*Second Witness*):

Q: You are the son of the plaintiff who was hit in the head with the baseball, correct?

A: Yes.

Q: Describe for us what happened?

A: My dad cried out, and I turned and he handed me a baseball.

Q: Did you see your dad get hit with the ball?

A: No.

Q: What did you do with the ball?

A: I have kept it in my possession since that time.

Q: Why did you do that?

A: Because I am a lawyer, and I thought that I might have a good lawsuit.

Q: How did you keep it?

A: Well, I carried it home with me.

Q: Then what did you do with it?

A: I locked it in my desk drawer and put the key on a chain and carried it around my neck.

Q: Does anyone else have a key to your desk drawer?

A: No.

Q: When did you remove the baseball?

A: I took the key from around my neck today, removed the baseball, and brought it with me to court.

Q: Do you have that baseball with you right now?

A: Yes, I do.

Q: Will you hand it to me, please?

A: Yes.

Q: I am showing you what has been marked for identification as Plaintiff's Exhibit No. 1. What is it?

A: It is the baseball that I kept in my possession since my dad gave it to me, that I just took out of my pocket and gave to you.

Q: By the way, how did Casey do that day?

A: He struck out.

Sample Dialogue

This example deals with an exhibit that cannot be specifically identified but which has not been tampered with because it has been kept in a sealed container.

Direct Examiner:

Q: What were you doing September 5, twenty years ago?

A: I was in my dorm room with a professor.

Q: What was his name?

A: Professor Kingsfield.

Q: What were you doing?

A: We were smoking marijuana.

Q: What did you do after you smoked the marijuana?

A: I picked up this partially smoked marijuana cigarette that had been smoked by the professor.

Q: What did you do with it?

A: I placed it in a standard letter-sized envelope, sealed the flap, wrote my name over the seal, and the date and the time.

Q: Why did you do that?

A: Well, I thought that some day Professor Kingsfield might be up for an appointment to the World Court.

Q: I am showing you what has been marked for identification as Plaintiff's Exhibit No. 1. Do you recognize it?

A: I do.

Q: What is it?

A: It is the envelope upon which I wrote my name and the date and the time twenty years ago after putting in the marijuana cigarette.

Q: What did you do with this envelope, Plaintiff's Exhibit No. 1?

A: I placed it in a box in my house in the attic.

Q: Where has Plaintiff's Exhibit No. 1 been for the past twenty years?

A: In that box in my house in the attic.

Q: Has the envelope been opened?

A: No, it has not.

Q: How do you know?

A: It is still sealed and has my name over the flap. The envelope is intact.

4.11   Limiting an Exhibit's Purpose

An exhibit, like any other form of evidence, may be admitted for a limited purpose. Federal Rule of Evidence 105 and similar state rules authorize evidence to be offered for a limited purpose. The contents of some exhibits may be admissible for one purpose but inadmissible for other purposes. In these situations, the offering advocate should indicate the limited purpose the exhibit serves. In a jury trial, it may be most critical that the fact finder receive precise instructions concerning the limited purpose of the exhibit.

Sample Dialogue

Assume the plaintiff has testified the injuries she sustained in a rollerblade accident due to the defendant's negligence have caused her to lose physical control over her arm and she is now unable to write. A defense witness has testified he saw the plaintiff write a note and this writing is being introduced as real evidence.

Defendant's Counsel:

     Your Honor, I offer Defense Exhibit No. 1.

The Court to Plaintiff's Counsel:

> Do you have any objections?

Plaintiff's Attorney:

> Not to the introduction to the exhibit, your Honor, but may we have an instruction to the jury that Defense Exhibit No. 1 is being offered for a limited purpose.

Judge:

> Yes, you may. (To the jury): Members of the Jury, I am instructing you at this time that Defense Exhibit No. 1 is being offered for the limited purpose to show that the plaintiff wrote a note. The actual words are not evidence in this case and should not be considered by you as such.

Sample Dialogue

Assume the defendant consumer testified that he paid for repairs done to his Sportster motorcycle and he has identified a $275 repair bill, Defendant's Exhibit No. 2, as the copy of the bill that he received marked "Paid."

Defendant's Counsel:

> I offer Defendant's Exhibit No. 2 into evidence for the limited purpose of proving that the defendant paid this bill.

Plaintiff's Attorney:

> Objection, your Honor. This bill contains hearsay information that repairs were done on the defendant's motorcycle and is inadmissible.

Defendant's Counsel:

> Your Honor, we do not offer the bill to prove the repairs were performed, but only to prove that the defendant paid money and received a receipt.

Judge:

> Objection overruled. Defendant's Exhibit No. 2 is received for the limited purpose explained by counsel.

4.12 Redacting an Exhibit

Some exhibit documents contain admissible and inadmissible evidence. The examining advocate should offer only those parts of the documents that are clearly admissible. When an objection to part of a document is sustained, the ruling will require that the inadmissible portions of the document be redacted (removed). The examining attorney may anticipate such objections and prepare an alternate exhibit which does not contain the inadmissible statements.

Sample Dialogue

Examining Advocate:

> Your Honor, we offer Plaintiff's Exhibit No. 12 into evidence which is a copy of the manuscript, *Paradise Regained,* written by John Milton. My client, the plaintiff, wrote some comments in the margins which contain statements that are irrelevant to this case. The other side has seen those comments and agrees with us that they are inadmissible. We eliminated those comments from this exhibit manuscript by whiting them out.

Opposing Advocate:

> Your Honor, we have no objection to the admissibility of Plaintiff's Exhibit No. 12 with those comments removed.

Judge:

> Plaintiff's Exhibit No. 12 is received.

There are a number of ways that inadmissible portions of a document may be eliminated. If only a few words or phrases need to be redacted, they may be easily obliterated by using white-out or a marking pen. If substantial portions of a document need to be deleted, those parts can be covered up with a piece of paper and a copy made of the document, with the copy containing only the admissible portions of the document admitted into evidence. If the form of the document is unimportant, the admissible portion of the contents may be retyped or recreated on a blank page and that new document admitted into evidence.

Sample Dialogue

Examining Attorney:

> Your Honor, we offer Plaintiff's Exhibit No. 7, a dental report prepared by the plaintiff's dentist, Dr. Olivier, into evidence.

Opposing Counsel (*At the bench*):

> Your Honor, we object to the second and third sentence of the first paragraph of the report. Those sentences contain statements that are inadmissible hearsay because they were not made to the doctor for purposes of diagnosis or treatment.

Judge:

> Sentences two and three of the first paragraph of Plaintiff's Exhibit No. 7 are ruled inadmissible. The remainder of the exhibit is received into evidence. Counsel, before you may show this exhibit to the jurors, you must remove those two sentences.

Examining Attorney (*At the bench*):

> Yes, your Honor. We will white them out.

Opposing Counsel (*At the bench*):

> Your Honor, we ask the court to instruct the jurors to disregard that portion of the dental record that is removed and that they not guess about what was contained in the document.

Judge:

> Members of the Jury, you may review the dental record of the plaintiff, but you are not to consider those statements that were omitted. You are to disregard them and not draw any inference or guess what was included in the document or why it was removed.

D. INTRODUCING EXHIBITS

4.13　What to Say

Many exhibits require the examiner to use precise legal terminology for their introduction and use. Specific questions, which may be artificial and formalistic, must be asked to establish the proper foundation. Most witnesses would never be able to come up with these words by themselves, and so the advocate is allowed—and required in many situations—to state the foundation words in the form of leading questions. This "litany" of questions elicits the precise elements of foundation necessary for the introduction and use of exhibits and reduces the time a witness would need to testify to such matters if leading questions were not used.

Sample Dialogue

Q:　Is this photograph a fair and accurate representation of the scene as you saw it on February 14, Ms. Valentine?

Q:　Are these records made in the ordinary and regular course of your travel business, Mr. Gulliver?

Q:　Is this musket in substantially the same condition as it was the day you first saw it at the scene of the shooting, Mr. Crockett?

4.14　Steps for the Admissibility of Exhibits

The introduction of exhibits requires several steps that the attorney should master and commit to memory. The witness must provide testimony which establishes the necessary foundation for the particular exhibit. While the precise steps vary from proceeding to proceeding and from exhibit to exhibit (depending on the particular exhibit's characteristics), the following steps provide a general format:

1. Qualify the witness by laying the *foundation* for the witness to identify the exhibit.

2. Make certain the exhibit has been pre-marked before the case or before the witness testifies, or have the item *marked* as an exhibit during the examination.

3. Ask permission to *approach the witness.* Many judges do not require this.

4. Request that the witness *examine* and *recognize* the exhibit.

5. Have the witness *identify* the exhibit.

6. *Offer* the exhibit into evidence by referring to its exhibit number or letter.

7. Provide the *opposing advocate* the opportunity to *review* the exhibit, if not done previously.

8. *Respond to* any *objections* made by the opposing advocate if necessary.

9. Obtain a *ruling.*

10. *Show* the exhibit *to* the *fact finder,* if admitted.

4.15 Illustration of How and When to Say What

Q: What is your name, sir?

A: Mr. Little.

Q: Where were you last June 1 at 3 o'clock in the afternoon?

A: Out in the chicken yard.

Q: What happened?

1. FOUNDATION

A: A brick fell into my yard and nearly hit me.

Q: What did you do?

A: I picked it up.

Q: Why?

A: I thought the sky was falling.

Q: What did you do with the brick you had picked up?

A: I scratched my name on it with a nail.

2. MARKED

To the Reporter:

May I have this marked for identification as Plaintiff's Exhibit No. 1?

Reporter:

Your exhibit has been marked for identification as Plaintiff's Exhibit No. 1.

3. APPROACH

To the Judge:

May I approach the witness?

Judge:

Yes, you may.

4. EXAMINE AND RECOGNIZE

Q: I have just handed you a brick which has been marked for identification as Plaintiff's Exhibit No. 1. Do you recognize it?

A: Yes.

Q: How?

A: I recognize the size and the shape and I recognize my name that I scratched on it with a nail.

5. IDENTIFY

Q: What is Plaintiff's Exhibit No. 1 for identification?

A: The object that fell in my yard last June 1.

Q: Is Plaintiff's Exhibit No. 1 for identification in the same condition as it was last June 1?

A: Yes.

6 & 7. OFFER AND REVIEW

To the Judge:

> At this time I offer Plaintiff's Exhibit No. 1. I am giving Plaintiff's Exhibit No. 1 to opposing counsel.

8. RESPONSE

Opposing Advocate:

> No objection.

9. RULING

Judge:

> Plaintiff's Exhibit No. 1 is admitted.

10. SHOW TO FACT FINDER

Plaintiff's Advocate:

> May the brick be shown to the jurors?

or

(To Judge or Arbitrator):

> Would you care to examine the exhibit at this time?

Judge/Arbitrator:

> Yes.

The following paragraphs explain each of these steps in detail.

4.15.1 Establishing Foundation for the Exhibit

Questions need to be asked of the witness to lay the foundation for the witness to identify the exhibit. The witness' testimony regarding the existence of the relevant exhibit is usually sufficient to establish this qualification.

Sample Dialogue

Q: What happened after the conference?

A: I signed the pact, and I saw Mr. Chamberlain sign the pact.

4.15.2 Marking the Exhibit

Most exhibits will be pre-marked before the case to some time during the proceeding or before the witness testifies. In a situation where an exhibit is not pre-marked, it can be marked during the proceeding. Exhibits will be marked either by a number or a letter. For example, all of the plaintiff's exhibits may be marked with numbers and the defendant's exhibits with letters. The reporter will know the proper system, and the advocate need not suggest to the reporter whether and what number or letter should be used.

4.15.3 Approaching the Witness

Some judges and arbitrators require the advocate to request permission before approaching the witness with an exhibit. Some expect them to seek such permission only with the first exhibit, or the first witness. Others do not require or expect the advocate to ask for such permission, because they recognize the advocate must approach the witness in order to show the exhibit to the witness. The advocate can ask about the preferred practice if uncertain whether a request should or need be made.

4.15.4 Examination and Recognition of Exhibit by the Witness

The advocate needs to describe on the record the actual handing of the exhibit to the witness. The advocate should always clearly refer to the number or letter marked on the exhibit to identify the exhibit for the record. There are a number of alternative phrases that may be used.

141

Examples

I am handing you what has been marked as Plaintiff's Exhibit No. 1 for identification.

You have in your hands . . . .

I hand you . . . .

I have just handed you . . . .

Here is . . . .

I show you . . . .

I am showing you . . . .

Grab this thing before I drop it . . . oops . . . .

The witness must be able to recognize the exhibit and explain how the witness is able to do so.

Sample Dialogue

Q: Do you recognize the Plaintiff's Exhibit No. 6 for identification Mr. Kane?

A: Yes.

Q: How?

A: I recognize the shape and color of the sled, of course, but I also recognize the word "Rosebud" on it.

Some judges and arbitrators require all references to an exhibit not yet received in evidence include the phrase "marked for identification." Most judges consider this an unnecessary, formalistic technicality and do not require the use of this phrase.

With some exhibits the advocate may appropriately describe the exhibit when it is handed to the witness. If it is obvious to everyone in the courtroom what the exhibit is, or if the identification of the exhibit is not in issue, the advocate may generically describe the exhibit.

Examples

Q: I hand you what has been marked as Plaintiff's Exhibit No. 2. Do you recognize this telescope, Mr. Galileo?

Q: Here is Plaintiff's Exhibit No. 3. It is a piece of paper with typing on it. Are you familiar with it, Ms. Street?

4.15.5 Identification of Exhibit by the Witness

The witness identifies the exhibit with a brief description of the exhibit.

Example

Q: Please look at Defense Exhibit C for identification, Mr. Daguerre, and tell us what it is.

A: It is a photograph I took of the Cathedral of Notre Dame de Paris.

Example

Q: Mr. Fitzgerald, what is Plaintiff's Exhibit No. 3?

A: It is a letter I received from Zelda.

It is improper for the advocate to describe an exhibit which is not identifiable by sight or is an issue in controversy.

Example

Direct Examiner:

Q: I show you Defendant's Exhibit No. 1, which is a letter signed by Howard Hughes.

Opposing Advocate:

Objection, your Honor. The exhibit may not be described as there is no foundation as to what that exhibit is.

Judge:

Objection sustained.

4.15.6   Offering the Exhibit Into Evidence

The advocate must offer the exhibit into evidence by referring to the exhibit by the assigned number or letter.

Example

I offer Plaintiff's Exhibit No. 1 into evidence.

Example

Defendant offers Exhibit E..

The advocate should avoid using unnecessary words in making the offer. It is not necessary to say "I would like to offer into evidence" because what the advocate "would like" to do is irrelevant. It is also unnecessary to make the request overly lengthy, such as "Your Honor, at this time, plaintiff requests this court rule that Plaintiff's Exhibit No. 132,641, which we offer into evidence is admissible, subject, of course, to any objection that counsel may make up." A short, simple declarative statement is sufficient.

4.15.7   Examination of the Exhibit by Opposing Counsel

After the exhibit is offered by the proponent, the opposing advocate may object to its admission. The opposing advocate must usually wait until the proponent has offered the evidence before an objection regarding admissibility can be made, unless there is a reason for making an earlier objection. Early objections to the admissibility of an exhibit may be made through a motion in limine. The opponent may also need to object to an exhibit if displaying it is unfairly prejudicial or otherwise objectionable, or if the examining advocate asks improper questions in an effort to lay a foundation for the introduction of the exhibit.

Some advocates show the exhibit to the opponent at the same time they offer the exhibit into evidence. They may walk over to the opponent's table and hand it to the opponent if the examining advocate wants the opposing advocate to look at the exhibit, or if the opposing advocate wants to look at the exhibit. It may be unnecessary to show the exhibit to the opponent because of the opponent's familiarity with the exhibit. In some jurisdictions the exhibit may be shown to the opposing advocate at an earlier time. The exhibit may be shown to the opponent before it is shown to the witness or the exhibit may be shown to the opponent after it is shown to the witness but before it is offered in evidence and shown to the fact finder.

4.15.8 Responding to Objections

The examining advocate may need to respond to any objections which the opponent has made to the introduction of the exhibit. If an objection is sustained, the examiner should ask additional questions to remedy the evidentiary deficiency, or should make an offer of proof.

4.15.9 Showing the Exhibit to the Fact Finder

How an exhibit is shown to the fact finder depends upon the type of exhibit, the exhibit's importance to the case, and how the offering the advocate wants to present the exhibit to the fact finder.

The offering attorney should provide the fact finder with sufficient time to understand, view or touch evidence before continuing with the examination of a witness or the introduction of other evidence.

There are a variety of ways documents may be shown to the fact finder. A document may be:

Read by the advocate or clerk (a neutral person).

Passed among the fact finders.

Copied, with one copy distributed to each fact finder.

Blown-up, placed on an easel, and explained by the witness.

Displayed by an overhead projector transparency.

Objects that are large, easily seen or dangerous need not be handed directly to the fact finder who can see these tangible objects while the witness is on the witness stand. Some tangible objects may need to be handled and individually seen by the fact finders.

Photographs and diagrams should be sufficiently large and clear to be seen by the fact finders. Color photographs, diagrams and charts will be more realistic, and distinctions more easily recognized. Slides, videos, computer graphics, and overhead projections along with photographs and charts must be displayed so the fact finders can see them easily so the witness and examiner can work with them and so the opponent is not blocked. The judge or arbitrator may also want to see the exhibit while it is being used. The advocate must know in advance the most effective way to use the room and must know the restrictions the judge or arbitrator may impose on placement.

How long an exhibit is displayed depends upon the type of exhibit. Items of real evidence are usually left on counsel table or on the clerk's table during the trial, unless their presence is unfairly prejudicial or otherwise objectionable. Demonstrative evidence is displayed during the testimony of a witness who uses the exhibit. If an opposing lawyer does not want the evidence to be displayed after the testimony of the witness, the opposing attorney may either physically move the exhibit, ask the examining attorney to put the exhibit away, or ask permission to have the exhibit removed. The same procedures are available for visual aids.

4.16 Using Stipulations

The advocates may stipulate to the foundation of an exhibit to avoid the need to ask detailed questions during the case. Stipulations can significantly reduce time and should be voluntarily entered into between counsel if there is no real dispute concerning the authenticity or accuracy of the exhibits. For example, hospital records will often be entered into evidence by stipulation because these records are usually reliable. A written stipulation should be introduced during the case, or an oral agreement summarized on the record. Stipulations regarding some facts are very common in bench trials and arbitrations. In jury trials, the offering advocate must request permission from the court to introduce the stipulation by reading it or have someone read the content of the stipulation.

Sample Dialogue

Plaintiff's Advocate:

> At this time I offer Plaintiff's Exhibit No. 53. It is an airplane sickness bag, the admissibility of which both Plaintiff Orville and Defendant Wilbur have agreed to through stipulation.

Judge (*To the Defense*):

> Is that correct?

Defendant's Advocate:

> Yes it is.

Judge:

> Plaintiff's Exhibit No. 53 is received.

Even when the opposition is likely to be cooperative and agree to stipulate to the admission of exhibits, there are occasions when laying the foundation is advantageous and may be important for persuasive foundation. In these situations, questions should be asked which establish a complete foundation for the exhibits. A proffered stipulation from the other side or urgings of the judge or arbitrator to accept such a stipulation may need to be resisted. In rejecting a stipulation, the examiner must decide that the laying of the foundation is strategically necessary for its persuasive value.

4.17 Admitting Pleadings, Claims, Responses, Admissions, and Discovery Responses

Pleadings, claim and response documents, and discovery documents are a part of the case but are not considered as evidence by the fact finder unless or until they are affirmatively offered as evidence during the case. The evidence may be offered during the direct or cross-examination of the witness who originally provided the information, or may be read during the offering party's case in chief or on cross examination.

Example

Plaintiff's Advocate:

> We offer Plaintiff's Exhibit No. 1, the letter containing the libelous statement made by the defendant about Oscar Wilde. The authenticity of the letter was admitted in Defendant's Answer, paragraph three, making it admissible.

Example

Defendant's Advocate:

> At this time I offer Defendant's Exhibit No. 25. It is a recipe by Mr. Huxtable that is in issue in this case, the admissibility of which has been obtained pursuant to Federal Rule of Civil Procedure 36. The admission can be found in Plaintiff's Response No. 4 to Defendant's Request for Admissions.

4.18 Abbreviating the Foundation

When there is a series of exhibits for which the foundations are similar the process of laying foundation after the first few exhibits have been introduced may be abbreviated. The witness can be asked whether the response given to the foundation questions for the previous exhibits would be essentially the same for subsequent exhibits which are to be introduced.

Sample Dialogue

Assume the witness has testified that he seized ten items from the defendant's garage. He has also testified when he seized these items, he used a marking pen to write his name, the date, and the time on each of the ten items.

Q: I am showing you what we have already marked for identification as Plaintiff's Exhibit No. 1. Do you recognize it?

A: Yes.

Q: How do you recognize it?

A: I recognize it by the fact my name, the date, and the time are written on the handle of the gun.

Q: It is Plaintiff's Exhibit No. 1 for identification?

A: It is the phazer gun I found in the defendant's garage.

Q: Where did you first see Plaintiff's Exhibit No. 1 for identification?

A: I saw it when I seized it from the defendant's garage.

Q: When did you put the markings on it?

A: At the time I seized it.

To the Judge:

    We offer Plaintiff's Exhibit No. 1.

Judge:

    With no objection, it is received.

Q: I am showing you what has been marked for identification as Plaintiff's Exhibit No. 2. It is a communicator. It has writing on the top in the surface of the plastic. Is that your writing?

A: Yes.

Q: Is that your name, the date, and the time?

A: Yes.

Q: Is that also an exhibit you found in the defendant's garage and marked in the same way as Plaintiff's Exhibit No. 1?

A: Yes.

And so on with the following eight exhibits.

4.19 Admitting Self-Authenticating Documents

S ome exhibits are self-authenticating. Federal Rule of Evidence 902 and similar state rules make it unnecessary to introduce evidence to authenticate certain exhibits including:

>Domestic public documents under seal.
>
>Domestic public documents not under seal.
>
>Foreign public documents.
>
>Certified copies of public documents.
>
>Official publications issued by public authorities.
>
>Newspapers and periodicals.
>
>Trade inscriptions.
>
>Acknowledged and notary public documents.
>
>Commercial paper and related documents.

After it is established that an exhibit falls into one of these categories, other evidence need not be introduced to establish its authenticity. The exhibit may be offered, unless some other evidence rule has not been met.

Sample Dialogue

To the Judge:

>I offer Plaintiff's Exhibit No. 5 for identification into evidence. It is a propeller blade. The blade has the tradename "Earhart" inscribed in the metal. The blade also has inscribed in the metal "Model 550." This exhibit is self-authenticating.

Judge:

>Received.

E. EVIDENTIARY FOUNDATION FOR VARIOUS EXHIBITS

T he necessary evidentiary foundation questions vary from exhibit to exhibit but, typically, responses are sought that establish the exhibit's existence, identity, authenticity, and accuracy. Because the legal grounds for admissibility must be met for each exhibit that is to be introduced, a checklist of foundation elements which sets out the necessary steps is helpful in introducing exhibits.

4.20 Physical Objects and Properties (Including Products, Clothing, and Weapons)

To admit a tangible object into evidence, the following elements must be proved:

The exhibit is relevant to the case.

The witness recognizes and can identify the exhibit.

The witness can recall what the exhibit looked like at the previous relevant time.

The exhibit is now in the same or substantially the same condition as when the witness saw it at the previous relevant time.

Sample Dialogue

Q: When you entered the Borden house, where did you go?

A: The bedroom.

Q: What did you see?

A: I saw an axe.

Q: Where was it?

A: On the floor.

Q: What did you do?

A: I picked it up.

Q: Why?

A: Because it was covered with blood.

Q: Was there anything else you noticed about the axe?

A: Yes, it had a chip on the handle.

Q: What did you do with it?

A: I took it back to the police department and put it in my evidence locker.

Q: How long was it there?

A: Until today.

Q: What did you do with it today?

A: I took it out of the evidence locker and brought it to court.

Q: Officer, I have just placed on the table in front of you what I have had marked for identification as State's Exhibit No. 1. It is an axe. Do you recognize it?

A: Yes.

Q: How do you recognize it?

A: I recognize the chip on the handle, the size, and the red stain.

Q: What is it?

A: It is the same axe I found in the living room of the Borden house.

Q: Does it appear to be in the same condition as it was when you picked it up?

A: Yes, except the red stain is now dry.

To the Judge:

Your Honor, I offer State's Exhibit No. 1 into evidence.

4.21 Documents (Including Letters, Contracts, Leases, and Other Signed Writings)

To admit documents into evidence the following elements must be proved:

The document is relevant to the case.

The document contains a signature, was handwritten, or bears some other identifying characteristics.

The signature, handwriting, or characteristic belongs to or identifies a person.

The witness saw the person sign or write the document; or

The witness knows, is familiar with, or can recognize the signature or handwriting; or

The witness recognizes and can identify the characteristics of the document; or

The witness is a party and admits signing, writing, or identifies the contents of the document; or

A handwriting expert states that the signature or writing is by a certain person or that the document can be identified by its characteristics.

The document is authentic.

The document is an original or an admissible duplicate or other copy.

The document is now in the same condition as when it was made and has not been altered.

Sample Dialogue (Letter)

Q: Mr. Abelard, do you know a woman by the name Heloise?

A: Yes.

Q: How do you know her?

A: We have been friends.

Q: How long?

A: We met twenty years ago. Then I went into a monastery and she went into a convent.

Q: How was your relationship continued?

A: Through letters over twenty years.

Q: How often did you correspond?

A: Frequently. Often on a weekly basis.

Q: Did you write to her?

A: Yes.

Q: Did she write to you?

A: Yes.

Q: Can you recognize her signature?

A: Of course.

Q: How?

A: Well, I had seen her sign her name before I went in the monastery, and I received hundreds of her letters over the past twenty years.

Q: I have just given you a piece of paper with handwriting
      on it which I have had marked for identification
      as Defendant's Exhibit No. 1. Do you recognize
      it?

A: Yes.

Q: How do you recognize it?

A: By the signature, Heloise, on the bottom, and by the
      date.

Q: What is it?

A: The last letter I received from Heloise.

To the Judge:

      I offer Defendant's Exhibit No. 1.

Sample Dialogue (Signed Document)

Q: Tell us your name please.

A: John Hancock.

Q: Where were you on July 4, 1776?

A: I was in Constitution Hall in Philadelphia.

Q: Why were you there?

A: To attend a meeting of the signing of the Declaration of
      Independence.

Q: Did you see the document being signed?

A: Yes.

Q: Whom did you see sign the Declaration?

A: Some other founding fathers and myself.

Q: Would you recognize the Declaration if you saw it again?

A: Yes.

Q: How?

A: By my signature on it, and I remember the words of the
      document.

Q: I have just given you what has been marked for
      identification as Defendant's Exhibit No. 6. Do
      you recognize it?

A: Yes.

Q: How?

A: I recognize the words and I recognize my signature.

Q: Your signature is rather large, isn't it?

A: Yes.

Q: How come?

A: I was feeling particularly revolutionary that day.

Q: Would you tell us please, what is Defendant's Exhibit No. 6?

A: It is the same Declaration of Independence that I and others signed on July 4, 1776.

Q: Has it been changed or altered in any way?

A: No.

To the Judge:

I offer Defendant's Exhibit No. 6.

Sample Dialogue (Contract)

Q: You said you entered into what you thought was a contract for employment as a first year associate?

A: Yes, I did.

Q: Did you negotiate that contract?

A: Yes, I did.

Q: With whom?

A: Brachman, the senior partner of the law firm.

Q: What term or terms did you negotiate?

A: The starting salary.

Q: How much was that for?

A: $100,147 a year. The last three digits were my LSAT score.

Q: Did you sign the contract?

A: Yes.

Q: Who else did?

A: Brachman.

Q: I have just handed you what I have marked for identification as Plaintiff's Exhibit No. 25. It is a piece of paper. Do you recognize it?

A: Yes, I do.

Q: How do you recognize it?

A: I recognize the signature of Brachman, the senior partner, my signature, and the contents.

Q: Have there been any additions or subtractions to that piece of paper since you signed it at the office of the senior partner?

A: No.

Q: What is Plaintiff's Exhibit No. 25 for identification?

A: It is the contract that I signed last year on April 18.

To the Judge:

I offer Plaintiff's Exhibit No. 25.

4.22 Business Correspondence (Including Letters, Memos, and Notes)

Business correspondence has similar foundation requirements as documents. Some correspondence may require additional foundation evidence to prove it was sent or received. In these instances, the additional elements include:

The correspondence was addressed to a certain person.

The witness saw or signed the original and any carbon or photocopy of the original.

The witness placed the correspondence in an accurately addressed delivery envelope; or the witness supervised a person who in the normal course of business mails such correspondence.

The envelope was placed in a mailbox or given to another carrier; or the witness supervised a person who in the normal course of business mails such envelopes.

The photocopy or carbon of the original is an accurate duplicate.

The original correspondence was received by the addressee or never returned to the sender.

Sample Dialogue (Memo)

Q: Tell us your name.

A: Colonel Tom Parker.

Q: For whom did you work in the summer of 1993?

A: Elvis Presley.

Q: What did you do?

A: I was his business manager.

Q: You are holding a piece of paper which has been marked for identification as Defendant's Exhibit No. 3. Do you recognize it?

A: Yes, I do.

Q: How do you recognize it?

A: I typed it, and I remember the words. These are my initials on the bottom, and I recognize Mr. Presley's signature.

Q: How?

A: I have seen him sign his name hundreds of times.

Q: What is Defendant's Exhibit No. 3?

A: It is a memo suggesting a personal interview that I typed for Elvis Presley which he signed and I mailed in the summer of 1993.

Q: Do you remember what you did with that paper that you typed after it had been signed by Elvis?

A: Yes. I mailed it.

Q: How did you mail the memo?

A: I placed it in an envelope and sealed the envelope.

Q: Did the envelope have any writing on it?

A: Yes.

Q: What was the writing?

A: It was addressed to: Publisher, National Enquirer.

Q: Do you know how the address got on there?

A: Yes.

Q: How?

A: I typed it on myself before I placed the memo in it.

Q: What did you do next?

A: I licked the stamp and put it in the upper right-hand corner.

Q: Then what did you do?

A: I walked outside to a mailbox.

Q: Then what?

A: I dropped it in the mailbox and went back to work.

Q: Did you ever get the envelope and memo returned to you?

A: No. Never.

To the Judge:

I offer Defendant's Exhibit No. 3.

Sample Dialogue (Oral contract reduced to writing)

Q: On March 2, Sir, in the year 2000, did you receive a phone call about 4:00 p.m.?

A: Yes.

Q: Did the caller identify himself or herself?

A: Yes.

Q: What did the caller say?

A: The caller said that he worked for the husband of the President. He said that the First Gentleman had a workshop in the basement of the White House and the First Gentleman wanted to start making small birdhouses and bird feeders to be distributed to nature centers throughout the country as a sign of his support for those societies.

Q: Did he say anything else?

A: Yes. He said he wanted to order a digital force power steel fastener implanter.

Q: What do you do for a living, sir?

A: I manufacture hammers.

Q: What did you do next?

A: I told him I needed an order in writing from the person ordering the goods from my company.

Q: Did you talk about anything else?

A: Yes. The caller told me that he was willing to pay up to $950.00 for the tool.

Q: What happened then?

A: Well, I was kind of excited because our usual hammer
      sells for $12.00. At that time, in anticipation of
      the letter, I set our design staff working on a
      model hammer.

Q: Did you ever receive any orders?

A: Yes. One week later I received a letter.

Q: Showing what I've marked for identification as Plaintiff's
      Exhibit No. 1, do you recognize that?

A: Yes, I do.

Q: How do you recognize it?

A: Well, it has a White House label and it says from the
      office of the First Gentleman and is signed with
      the name of the First Gentleman.

Q: Anything else?

A: Yes. It is an order for a digital force power steel fastener
      implanter.

To the Judge:

We offer Plaintiff's Exhibit No. 1.

Judge:

It is received.

Examiner:

Q: What did you do after that?

A: Well, we worked for a couple weeks and came up with a
      modified new hammer model. We packaged
      this hammer in a box and included a letter of
      acceptance and a bill for $723.33.

Q: How did you do the mailing?

A: I addressed the package to the First Gentleman at the
      White House and put some stamps on it. Then I
      put it in the "out" basket on my desk.

Q: What is the mailing procedure in your office?

A: Our company procedure is that all mail is picked up
      periodically by our messenger. He goes through
      all the offices, picks up all the mail from the
      "out" baskets and mails it.

Q: Did you ever notice in your "out" basket that the package was no longer there?

A: Yes, I did. Later that same day, my "out" basket was empty.

Q: I am showing you what has been marked for identification as Plaintiff's Exhibit No. 2. Do you recognize this?

A: Yes, I do.

Q: How?

A: By its contents.

Q: What is it?

A: Exhibit No. 2 is a copy of the letter that I sent to the First Gentleman along with the hammer.

Q: Who made the copy?

A: I did.

Q: Why did you do that?

A: Well, as a matter of policy in our business, whenever anyone writes a letter a copy is made. I put this copy in my contract file. I recognize this exhibit as an exact copy of the letter that I wrote, signed, and placed in the package that was sent.

To the Judge:

At this time plaintiff offers Exhibit No. 2.

4.23 Business Records (Including Memoranda, Reports, Writings, or Data Compilations)

Records maintained in the ordinary course of business may be introduced through a witness who does not have personal knowledge of the recorded information but does have personal knowledge concerning the business recording process. The introduction of this information is allowed by the foundation elements detailed in Federal Rule of Evidence 803(6) and similar state rules. The term "business" includes any business, hospital, institution, organization, association, profession, occupation, and calling of any kind including nonprofit agencies. The content of business records may include facts,

acts, events, conditions, opinions or diagnoses that are relevant to the case. The elements to be proved under Federal Rule of Evidence 803(6) include:

The report must have been "made at or near the time" of the occurrence which gave rise to the report.

The record was made by "a person with knowledge" of the information or was made "from information transmitted by" a person with knowledge.

The record was made "in the regular practice of that business activity."

The record was kept "in the course of a regularly conducted business activity."

The witness is the "custodian" of the documents or is in some other way a "qualified witness."

Sample Dialogue (Hospital Records)

Q: What is your name, sir?

A: Charles Drew.

Q: Where do you work?

A: Metropolitan Medical Center.

Q: What is your job?

A: I am the medical records librarian.

Q: As a medical records librarian, what do you do?

A: I am the custodian in charge of all the hospital records of the Metropolitan Medical Center.

Q: Do you have a staff working for you?

A: Yes. They all work at my direction and control.

Q: Do you have a policy in your hospital concerning the making of records?

A: Yes, we do.

Q: What is that policy?

A: All medical records must have been made at or near the time of the occurrence of the information contained in them. The record must be made by a person with knowledge of the information or was made from information given to that person by someone with knowledge.

Q: I am showing you what has been already marked for identification as Plaintiff's Exhibit No. 23. Can you tell us what it is?

A: Yes, they are medical records obtained from our medical records library of a patient with the patient number 2345, which corresponds with the name Mabel Stampers.

Q: Are these records kept under your control?

A: Yes.

Q: You reviewed these records?

A: Yes.

Q: Viewing these records, did you determine whether these records have been made at or near the time of the occurrence of the information contained in it?

A: Yes, they were.

Q: How do you know that?

A: The different occurrences are dated and timed and the time of the dictation of the information is also dated. My examination of both the record and the dictation notes shows that they were made at or near the time of the occurrence.

Q: Looking at these records, can you determine whether the record was made by a person who had knowledge of the information contained in the records?

A: Yes, I can.

Q: How?

A: In each of these cases the person making the dictation was a doctor, and the doctor was assigned to the case by patient name and number.

Q: Are these records kept in the course of the regularly conducted business of your hospital?

A: Yes, they are.

Q: Was this record made in the regular practice of that business or hospital activity?

A: Yes, it was.

To the Judge:

       I offer Plaintiff's Exhibit No. 23.

Computer printouts may or may not qualify as business records. When computer records will not qualify as business records, additional foundational questions relating to the input, storage, and retrieval methods of the computer system and its reliability will be necessary.

Sample Dialogue (Computer Data)

Q: Ms. Lopez, at Fidelity Finance Company has it been the regular practice that a person with knowledge of the data enters that information on computer?

A: Yes.

Q: As custodian of Fidelity's computer records are you familiar with the method of entry, storage, and retrieval of data in the system?

A: Yes, I am.

Q: Is that system reliable?

A: Yes.

Q: Are there safeguards capable of detecting and correcting errors in the system?

A: There are.

Q: Does the computer printout reliably contain the retrieved data?

A: Yes.

Q: Is the information necessary for notices of delinquent accounts programmed into the computer at or near the time invoices are sent out?

A: Yes, on the first working day of each month.

Q: Do you know Fidelity's procedure for keeping records of the delinquent accounts and its notifying customers in default in March, 1989?

A: Yes.

Q: Please explain those default and notification procedures.

A: The data reflecting all activity on the account are verified by hand. Then the verified data is keyed into the terminal and copied on magnetic tape. Every working day the magnetic tape merges the new data with the information already on the accounts record for the month. The computer, by the 15th of the month, finds all accounts not currently paid. To find these accounts, the computer uses instructions from a program to search and identify delinquent accounts. As instructed, the computer prints up these accounts. This printout is held five days. If the account is paid up within that time, no additional interest is assessed, but additional interest is assessed if the account remains unpaid. As programmed, all the accounts, delinquent or otherwise, are put into monthly statement form. Using the program, the computer prints the statement for each Fidelity Finance account, prints out the next payment's due date, folds, and stuffs the statement into a window envelope, meters the letter for first-class mailing, seals the envelope, and lines the envelope up in trays for delivery to the post office. Hundreds of thousands of accounts are handled like this every month.

Q: What steps does Fidelity take to ensure the computer finds and identifies delinquent accounts so accurate notices of default notify customers?

A: Special control procedures are built into the system. Transcriptions of data are verified by two different terminal operators. In the computer the two sets of data are verified. Accounts identified as unpaid by the 15th are rechecked. If these accounts remain unpaid during the next five days, notices are printed and included with the statement, folded, put in a window envelope with Fidelity's return address for return delivery.

Q: I'm showing you what's been marked Defendant's Exhibit No. 8. What it is?

A: It's Mr. Genander's delinquency notice from Fidelity Finance.

Q: How do you recognize it?

A: This is a duplicate of the statement on our computer system.

Q: Was this duplicate printed in the regular course of business?

A: Yes.

Q: Was this notice and statement prepared by the computer system and program you have described for us this afternoon?

A: Yes.

Q: Is the information on Exhibit No. 8 correct?

A: It is correct for the date stated.

To the Judge:

I offer Defendant's Exhibit No. 8.

Opponent:

May I examine the witness for the purpose of laying a foundation for an objection?

Judge:

Yes, you may.

Opponent:

Q: Ms. Lopez, Defendant's Exhibit No. 8 was printed up on March 20 of last year, wasn't it?

A: Yes.

Q: You did not make any data entry on this statement and notice of delinquency from which Exhibit No. 8, the printout was made, did you?

A: No. The accounts receivable operators and the computer system read the data, and the computer program carries out the accounting procedure.

Q: Does the computer itself read documents like the statement printout, Exhibit No. 8?

A: Only if the computer is equipped with an optical scanner.

Q: But your computer does not have such a scanner, does it?

A: It does not.

Q: And your computer cannot read this statement, can it?

A: No, only the magnetic language it stores on the disk.

Q: How often does the computer put account information on magnetic tape?

A: Daily, but only on accounts that have had activity. The transcription of daily activity is run through the system to merge with the last cumulative tape. The computer, by program, performs the necessary accounting on active accounts and the cumulative tape is thus updated.

Q: Fidelity does not store all these updated tapes, do they?

A: No, the old cumulative tape is "written over." It becomes the current cumulative tape at the end of each business day. The tape remains the same, but the changes in accounts are reflected in the different magnetic code.

Q: So that Exhibit No. 8 was printed on one of these "written over" tapes?

A: Yes, it was.

Q: And the entries on the "written over" tape from which Exhibit No. 8 was printed were made on March 20 of last year?

A: Yes.

Q: The entry was made 36 months after Mr. Genander took out this loan from Fidelity?

A: Yes.

To the Judge:

I object, Exhibit No. 8 is hearsay. The witness admits no personal knowledge of input or retrieval.

Judge:

Overruled. The exhibit is a business record made by defendant's computer in the regular course of plaintiff's business. Defendant's Exhibit No. 8 is received.

4.24 Copies

Modern copying equipment creates accurate copies of original documents and records. These "duplicate" originals are admissible. However, the original may be the most persuasive and, if available, should be offered to prove its content. See Fed.R.Evid. 1002. A duplicate original may be routinely admitted unless it is of questionable authenticity or it would be unfair to admit a copy. See Fed.R.Evid. 1003. A copy may also be admissible if the original has been lost or destroyed, is in the possession of the opponent, or is otherwise not obtainable. See Fed.R.Evid. 1004.

Sample Dialogue

(The witness has testified that he saw and read the original agreement):

Q: Brother Timothy, I am showing you Defendant's Exhibit No. 23 marked for identification. Do you recognize it?

A: Yes.

Q: What is it?

A: It is a copy of the rental agreement for the monastery.

Q: How do you know?

A: I recognize all the words and terms.

Q: Do you have the original?

A: No.

Q: Was this copy made from the original?

A: Yes.

Q: How do you know?

A: I saw the landlord use his office photocopy machine right after I signed the original lease. The landlord handed me the copy, and I saw the landlord put the original in a filing cabinet. I brought this copy home and put it in the monastery vault.

Q: Has it changed in any way?

A: No.

Q: Is this the copy, Defendant's Exhibit No. 23, that you removed from your vault?

A: Yes.

To the Judge:

I offer Defendant's Exhibit No. 23.

4.25 Electronic Recordings (Including Audio and Video Recordings)

The elements necessary to establish a sufficient foundation for the introduction of recordings are:

The electronic recording is relevant to the case.

The operator of the equipment was qualified to run the equipment.

The recording equipment was checked before its use and operated normally.

The witness heard or saw the event being electronically recorded.

After the event had been recorded, the witness reviewed the tape and determined that it had accurately and completely recorded the event.

The witness can recognize and identify the sounds or images on the recording.

The recording is in the exact same condition at the time of case as it was at the time of the taping.

Sample Dialogue (Video Event)

Q: Sheriff, where were you on the 24th day of November, 1963?

A: I was in the Dallas jail.

Q: Where in the Dallas jail?

A: I was in the basement garage by the exit ramp.

Q: What did you see?

A: I saw a man that I later learned was Jack Ruby point a gun in the direction of Lee Harvey Oswald and shoot at him.

Q: Sheriff, I have given you a videotape which has been marked for identification as Plaintiff's Exhibit No. 155. Do you recognize it?

A: Yes, I do.

Q: How do you recognize it?

A: Well, I wrote my initials on the label of the tape that I saw before coming into this courtroom today. After I saw it, I also wrote my initials on this card which indicates that I have seen the tape.

Q: What is on the tape?

A: It's a tape of what I just described . . . of the shooting I saw on the 24th day of November in 1963.

Q: Is this videotape a complete and accurate representation of what you saw that day?

A: Yes, it is.

To the Judge:

I offer Plaintiff's Exhibit No. 155.

Sample Dialogue (Sound Recording)

Q: Mr. Caul, what do you do for a living?

A: I install electronic sound recording instruments.

Q: Have you ever installed sound recording instruments for the President?

A: Yes, I have.

Q: When was that?

A: A short time before he left office.

Q: Where did you do the installation?

A: In the Oval Office of the White House.

Q: What did that consist of?

A: I set up a secret tape recording device in the desk in the Oval Office. I put the receiving device in another room.

Q: Did you ever test the device?

A: Yes, I did.

Q: How did you do that?

A: I started the machine running, went in the other room, and watched it record. It recorded for one hour.

Q: What did you do after that?

A: I removed the tape and played it on my tape player.

Q: Did you recognize the voice of anybody on the tape?

A: Yes.

Q: Whose?

A: I recognized the voice of the President.

Q: What did you do with the tape?

A: I took the tape and put it in a special envelope and sealed it, and I have kept it in my safe in my office until I brought it here to court.

Q: Did you listen to the tape before you came in here?

A: Yes.

Q: Whose voices are there?

A: There is only one voice.

Q: Whose voice is it?

A: The tape just contains the voice of the President.

Q: Have you made any additions or subtractions or changes to that tape?

A: No, I have not.

Q: You have in your hand Plaintiff's Exhibit No. 23. Do you recognize it?

A: Yes, that's the tape.

Q: How do you recognize it?

A: I removed it from the envelope that I had previously sealed.

Q: Was the envelope sealed at this time?

A: No, it was not. I opened it in the court's chambers before trial started and after that I gave it to you.

To the Judge:

I offer Plaintiff's Exhibit No. 23.

To Opponent:

This is the tape that we gave to you in discovery before this trial started.

Judge:

It is received.

Examiner:

May I play the tape at this time?

Judge:

Yes, you may.

4.26 Test Results (Including X-Ray Films and Laboratory Analysis)

Exhibits containing results from tests, x-rays, and other procedures require special foundation information. These are the elements to be proven:

The exhibit is relevant to the case.

The witness is qualified to operate the equipment.

There exists a procedure which regulates the testing, x-ray or analysis process.

The witness personally conducted or supervised an operator who conducted the testing, developed the x-rays or completed the analysis.

The equipment was in normal operating condition.

The witness can recognize and identify the results, x-rays or analysis.

The results, x-rays or analysis are in the same condition as when they were completed.

Sample Dialogue (X-ray)

Q: Mr. Igor, you are an x-ray technician employed by Share Health, aren't you?

A: Yes, I am.

Q: Were you on duty on Tuesday, July 3, at the Spring Lake Center Clinic?

A: Yes.

Q: Mr. Igor, I'm handing you what's been marked for identification as Plaintiff's Exhibit No. 2. Do you recognize it?

A: Yes, I do.

Q: What is it?

A: It's a flat plate abdominal x-ray I took on July 3 of last year.

Q: How do you know?

A: My initials, I.I., are in the corner next to the date and the patient's identifying number. That number is from the patient's chart, the medical record at Share Health.

Q: Mr. Igor, I'm handing you Plaintiff's Exhibit No. 1, already stipulated as Mr. Frankenstein's chart and received into evidence. What is the medical record number?

A: (*Reading*) 01–146203.

Q: Now I'm handing you what's been marked as Plaintiff's Exhibit No. 2, the x-ray. What number is it that indicates the patient's chart?

A: It's next to the date.

Q: What is that number?

A: (*Reading*) 01–146203.

Q: Are you a certified technician?

A: Yes.

Q: How did you prepare this x-ray?

A: I made the exposure.

Q: Was the machine functioning properly?

A: Yes, there was no problem.

Q: After you made the exposure, what did you do?

A: I developed it, put my ID, the date, and the patient's ID on it, then I printed it and sent it up to the radiologist to interpret.

To the Judge:

I offer Plaintiff's Exhibit No. 2.

4.27 Photographs (Including Prints, Slides, and Movies)

The use of photographs is an effective way of making the facts of a case real. The elements to be proven to admit photographs into evidence are:

The photograph is relevant to the case.

The witness is familiar with the scene displayed in the photograph at the relevant time of the event.

The photograph fairly and accurately depicts the scene at the time of the event.

Sample Dialogue (Photograph)

Q: Ms. Jetson, on July 1, 2988, at approximately 2:00
       sundial time, were you at the intersection of
       Lunar Pad and Galaxie Avenue?

A: Yes, I was.

Q: What were you doing there?

A: I was waiting for the space shuttle.

Q: While you were waiting for the shuttle, what did you
       observe?

A: I saw two cars, a Masarocket and a Lambomissle, enter
       the intersection and collide.

Q: I show you what has been marked as Defendant's
       Exhibit No. 1 for identification and ask you to
       examine it. Do you recognize it?

A: Yes, I do.

Q: What is it?

A: It's a photograph of the intersection where the accident
       occurred.

Q: Is the scene on the photograph in any way different
       from the scene that you observed on July 1,
       2993?

A: No.

Q: Is the photograph a fair and accurate depiction of the
       scene of the accident that you observed on July
       1.

A: Yes, it is.

To the Judge:

       I offer Defendant's Exhibit No. 1.

There is no need to establish the type of camera used, film
speed, focal lens, shutter speed, lens opening, other photogra-
phy details, or even when the picture was taken, unless these
facts are an issue in a case.

4.28 Demonstrative Evidence

Various types of demonstrative evidence may be useful during the presentation of a case. The elements to be proven in order to establish the foundation for the introduction of a diagram are:

The witness is familiar with the scene or event.

The witness recognizes the scene depicted in the diagram or is familiar with the exhibit.

The demonstrative exhibit will assist the witness in explaining testimony and will aid the fact finder in understanding the testimony.

The demonstrative evidence is reasonably accurate (even if not to scale) and is not misleading.

Sample Dialogue (Prepared Diagram)

Q: Ms. Monroe, are you familiar with the intersection of Hollywood and Vine in Hollywood, California?

A: Yes, I am.

Q: Do you remember what the intersection looked like on April 4, four years ago?

A: Yes, I do.

Q: How do you remember?

A: That was the day that as I was leaving the drugstore I saw an accident.

To the Judge:

May I approach the witness?

Judge:

Yes, you may.

Examiner:

Q: Ms. Monroe, I am showing you a diagram marked as Plaintiff's Exhibit No. 1 that has already been prepared. Have you seen it before?

A: Yes, I have.

Q: Is this diagram a fair and accurate representation of the
         location of the streets and the buildings at the
         intersection of Hollywood and Vine on April 4,
         four years ago?

A: Yes, it is.

Q: Would this diagram assist you in describing to the jury
         what you saw that day?

A: Yes, it would.

To the Judge:

         I offer Plaintiff's Exhibit No. 1 for demonstrative pur-
         poses.

Judge:

         It is received.

Examiner:

         May I place it on the easel and have the witness ap-
         proach the diagram?

Judge:

         Yes, you may.

Examiner:

Q: Ms. Monroe, there is an arrow on the diagram indicating
         north is to the top of the diagram. Is that
         correct?

A: Yes.

Q: Which way does Hollywood run?

A: It runs from north to south.

Q: And that is from top to bottom on the diagram?

A: Yes.

Q: Would you take the red marker and write your last name
         a bit to the right of where you were to show us
         where you were at that intersection when you
         saw the accident?

A: I was right here.

Q: You have written Monroe on the northeast corner of the
         intersection. Is that right?

A: Yes.

Q:	Now, what did you see?

A: I saw one car coming from the east and one car coming from the west, and they met head-on in the middle of the intersection.

Q: Did you learn who was driving the car from the east?

A: Yes, he told me his name was Clark.

Q: What about the car from the west?

A: The driver said his name was Paul.

Q: Will you label the car coming from the east, Clark, and the one from the west Paul in the center of the cars?

A: Yes.

Q: Will you draw a line from the cars from the east and west showing where they collided in the intersection?

A: Yes, I will.

Q: Will you mark with an "X" the spot of the crash?

A: All right.

To the Judge:

At this time I re-offer the exhibit as marked.

Judge:

It is once again received.

The advocate must permit the witness to explain what is occurring during the use of demonstrative evidence to make a clear record of the demonstrative evidence. The record should indicate what the demonstrative evidence is and how it is being used. The exhibit may be re-offered after the witness has written on it. This re-offer may prevent the opponent from writing on or erasing the markings because the exhibit is now in evidence as marked and should not be changed by the other side because the record of the actual exhibit should not be changed.

Sample Dialogue (Model)

Q: Dr. Pierce, did you have the opportunity to examine the knee of my client, Mr. Radar?

A: Yes, I did.

Q: Did you do any surgery on my client's knee?

A: Yes, I did.

Q: Would a model of a knee assist you in explaining to us what you saw during the visual and surgical examination of my client's knee?

A: Yes, it would.

Q: You have in your hand now what has been marked for identification as Plaintiff's Exhibit No. 1. What is it?

A: It is an anatomical model of a person's knee.

Q: Is that an exact model of a person's knee?

A: Yes, it is.

Sample Dialogue (Freehand Drawing)

Q: Now you said earlier that you have had an idea for some kind of cartoon character?

A: Yes, I did.

Q: What kind of character?

A: A rodent.

Q: Would it assist you in explaining your idea to us if you would go to the board and draw your idea on that board with this marker?

A: Yes, it would.

Q: Now sir, I see you have drawn some sort of mouse on the board.

A: It's a rodent.

Q: Are you sure that's a rodent, it looks like a rat?

A: It is a rodent.

Q: What are you drawing on the rodent?

A: Pants and shoes.

Q: And now what are you drawing?

A: Three-fingered gloves.

Q: Do you have a name for this character?

A: Yes, I do.

Q: And what is that name?

A: I have been thinking about Ralph.

Sample Dialogue (Computer Graphic)

Q: Dr. Lucas, after you examined all of the photographs, the movies and Nash Rambler four-wheel drive car, what did you do?

A: I read all of the statements and the accident reports.

Q: Then what did you do?

A: I read all of the scientific reports and conducted my own tests of the Nash Rambler.

Q: Then what?

A: I worked with a computer graphic artist and film maker to design a computer simulation of how the wheel bearings failed causing the wheel to come off and the Nash Rambler to roll over.

Q: Have you seen the computer simulation?

A: Yes.

Q: Based on all of the tests, the statements, and photographs and based on your scientific training and experience are you able to say if the simulation is a fair and accurate representation of what happened?

A: Yes, I am.

Q: Is it?

A: Yes.

Q: Would the simulation assist you in describing what happened?

A: It surely would.

To Judge:

At this time I offer defendant's exhibit No. 35. This is the computer simulation we showed you and the opponent before the hearing began today.

Judge:

> Exhibit No. 35 is received.

Examiner:

Q: Dr. Lucas, would you access the simulation on the computer next to you on the witness stand and explain the first thing we see?

A photograph may be taken of the information on the board and introduced into evidence as a part of the record when the board itself is not introduced.

The introduction and use of demonstrative evidence is subject to a variety of approaches depending upon the practice in a forum. In some tribunals, the examiner need not formally offer a demonstrative exhibit into evidence but need only ask permission for the witness to use the demonstrative exhibit. In these jurisdictions this permission makes the exhibit part of the record. In other tribunals, the demonstrative exhibit is not offered into evidence until after the witness has used it during testimony or has marked on it.

In cases where more than one witness uses or marks a demonstrative exhibit, the procedures for its introduction may also vary. If a second witness uses or marks the exhibit, the demonstrative evidence may have to be re-offered because new information now appears on the exhibit. The markings may be distinguished by the use of a different color marker or by the placement of a clear, plastic sheet over the drawing or chart which the witness draws on to distinguish those markings from the markings of the first witness.

4.29 Summary Exhibits

Summaries of evidence may be introduced as an efficient and effective means to explain evidence to the fact finder. Summary exhibits may include a chart detailing the testimony of one or more witnesses or a summary description of documents. Federal Rule of Evidence 1006 and similar state rules permit summaries of writings to be introduced as evidence. The elements for introduction of summaries include:

All the information summarized must be relevant.

The witness has knowledge concerning the information contained in the summary.

The witness has reviewed the exhibit and verified that it is an accurate summary of the evidence.

Sample Dialogue

Q: Now you have told us you recently graduated from law school and are a law clerk for our law firm?

A: Yes.

Q: What have you done in preparing this case for trial?

A: I have prepared an exhibit list of the 5,457 exhibits listing a brief description of the items that have been introduced in this trial and received by the court as having come from King Tut's tomb.

Q: I am showing you what has been marked for identification as Plaintiff's Exhibit No. 5458 which is a 50 page document with typing on each page. Are you familiar with this document?

A: Yes.

Q: How are you familiar with it?

A: I personally prepared the entire document.

Q: What is it?

A: It is a listing of all the exhibits, Nos. 1 through 5457 in this case, with a brief description of each of those exhibits.

Q: Is it a fair and accurate description of each one of the exhibits?

A: Yes.

To the Judge:

At this time we offer Plaintiff's Exhibit No. 5458, the exhibit summary of all the plaintiff's exhibits introduced into evidence.

4.30 Judicial, Administrative, and Arbitral Notice

A judge, administrative hearing officer, or arbitrator may take notice of facts, at any time during a proceeding, that are accurate, verifiable by reliable sources, and indisputable. See Fed.R.Evid. 201. Noticed facts may appear in an exhibit.

Sample Dialogue

To Judge:

It is critical to this case that we prove what day December 7, 1941 fell on, as well as the days of the week upon which other dates fell in 1941. I have marked a 1941 calendar as Plaintiff's Exhibit A for identification. At this time I request the court take judicial notice of the accuracy of this calendar and admit Plaintiff's Exhibit A into evidence.

Judge:

I will take notice of Plaintiff's Exhibit A and admit Exhibit A into evidence.

4.31 Past Recollection Recorded

A witness who, at the time of the proceeding, does not have an independent recollection of an event may have previously made a record of that event and that record may be introduced as an exhibit of real evidence. The elements to establish the foundation include:

The witness has no present recollection of the relevant event.

The witness once had knowledge of the event.

The witness made a record of the event when the matter was fresh in the witness' memory.

The recorded recollection accurately reflects the knowledge of the witness.

The exhibit is in the same condition now as when it was made.

Sample Dialogue (Lack of Memory)

Q: Mr. Gilligan, on February 18, 1968, do you remember what happened to you after you boarded the S.S. Minnow?

A: I was injured in a boating accident when the tiny ship was tossed, if not for the courage of the fearless crew the Minnow would have been lost.

Q: Do you remember any other details of that accident?

A: No, I do not. I have not been able to remember the details since the day after my accident.

Q: The day of the accident, did you give a statement to anyone?

A: Yes, I did.

Q: To whom did you give a statement?

A: I gave a statement to a coast guard officer.

Q: At the time you gave the statement, do you remember what details occurred to you at the accident?

A: Yes, I did.

Q: Do you have a memory of those details now?

A: I do not.

Q: At the time you gave the statement to the coast guard officer, what did you do?

A: I read it, and I signed it.

Q: Showing you what has been marked by the court reporter as Defendant's Exhibit No. 50—it's a three-page hand-written, water-stained statement with your signature on each page and the date, February 18, 1968—do you recognize this document?

A: Yes, I do.

Q: What is it?

A: It is a statement I wrote and signed the day of the accident.

Q: Would you please read the statement silently to yourself.

A: Yes.

Q: Having read the statement, does it refresh your
       recollection as to the details of what happened
       in the accident?

A: No, I really don't remember.

Q: Would you have signed this statement if it had not been
       accurate?

A: No, I would not have.

To the Judge:

At this time I offer Defendant's Exhibit No. 50 as
past recollection recorded.

Sample Dialogue (Detailed Facts)

Q: Ms. Ames, do you recall going to Van Line's warehouse
       on April 18 last year?

A: Yes, I do.

Q: And you accompanied Mr. Andrews, the defendant,
       who was inventorying the library shipped from
       his mother's Galveston, Texas home?

A: Yes.

Q: How did you assist Mr. Andrews?

A: As he opened each box and told me the contents and
       condition of each book, I used a dictaphone to
       record the information.

Q: Each box was inventoried?

A: Yes.

Q: What did you do after you completed the inventory?

A: We returned to the office, and I transcribed the tapes
       onto typewritten sheets.

Q: Do those typewritten sheets contain all the information
       from the tapes?

A: Yes, and they also include the value for each title based
       on its condition and rarity.

Q: When did you type in the value?

A: Thursday, after I typed the information. Mr. Andrews
       told me what value to put by each book, and I
       did so.

Q: Do you remember the valuation of the volumes written
         by Virginia Woolf?

A: Not really.

Q: Would it help you to look at the typewritten list where
         those editions are valued?

A: Yes, it would.

Q: Ms. Ames, here is Defendant's Exhibit E marked for
         identification. Do you recognize it?

A: Yes, this is the list I transcribed from the warehouse tapes
         and these are the values I typed in next to each
         title after Mr. Andrew's appraisal.

Q: Is the list in the same condition as it was when you
         typed it?

A: Yes, it looks the same.

To the Judge:

I offer Defendant's Exhibit E into evidence.

Judge:

Received.

Examiner:

Q: Ms. Ames, please read the Virginia Woolf titles and their
         value as set out on page four of that list.

4.32 Demonstrations

Live demonstrations or experiments are difficult and unpredictable. They may work well at rehearsal, but can fail too easily. An effective alternative is to prepare a videotape of the experiment or demonstration and if it works show it during the case.

A simple demonstration that can be easily performed may be conducted if appropriate. A witness who displays an injury or shows how an object was held can assist the fact finders in understanding what happened. Anything more complex should be videotaped before the case, or, if resources do not permit, not done at all.

Sample Dialogue

Q: Ms. Chiquita, where were you on March 10, two years ago?

A: I was in the produce department of the Foods Unlimited supermarket.

Q: Did anything happen to you there?

A: Yes.

Q: What?

A: I was walking down the aisle when I slipped on a banana peel that was lying on the floor.

Q: Did you see the banana peel before you slipped?

A: Yes.

Q: When?

A: Just as I stepped on it, I looked down and saw it under my left foot.

Q: What happened?

A: Both feet went out from under me. My feet went up in the air and I came down hard on my right elbow.

Q: What happened to you?

A: I felt terrible pain in my elbow and saw a bone sticking out of my arm and lots of blood.

Q: Would you be able to demonstrate how you fell in the store?

A: Yes.

Q: Would that assist you in explaining to us what happened?

A: Yes.

To The Judge:

     May the witness please step down from the stand and demonstrate to us what happened?

Opponent:

     I have absolutely no objections.

Judge:

     Go ahead counsel. If you insist, the witness can give it a try. This ought to be real interesting.

F. THE USE OF TECHNOLOGY

Modern technology now provides the capabilities to create and use innovative and persuasive exhibits to present information. The appropriate use of this technological wizardry may help educate and persuade the fact finder. Evidence can easily be retrieved and displayed during argument or testimony. Theme words, impact phrases and the law may be interspersed with real and demonstrative evidence. Excerpts from video depositions and movies may be used during summation.

Advances in technology provides tools to the advocate which are far more sophisticated and effective than chalk boards, flipcharts, and simple diagrams. The wonders of technology cause unbelievable flights of fancy. Computer games, simulations, and computer graphics can create whole new worlds previously existing only in imagination. The power to recreate an accident, or make it happen in different ways, the capability of creating and displaying acts and events, and the availability of computer exhibits cause advocates to develop cases around new technology.

The temptation to impress with technology rather than persuade with the facts is difficult to resist. But technology is not, and should not be, a substitute for a well told story. An inexpensive hardware store model and a straightforward story may have far more persuasive value than expensive and complex computer graphics or expensive models that are engineering masterpieces. Cost and time must be weighed against value. If the technology helps tell a good story, it should be used If not, if should be saved for Walt Disney. The fact finder should see the point not the technology.

In order to use technology effectively the advocate must consider both the design and the use of the technology. Articles and materials can be reviewed for ideas and approaches. Consultants, sales people, and colleagues can help in choosing the most effective methods. A technician can assist the advocate to assure everything is and stays operating.

Proper placement of the equipment, back-up machinery in case of failure, limitations placed on the presentation due to the hearing room space, the applicable rules of the forum, must all be considered in determining whether and how to use technology. The advocate must practice in order to be both comfortable and effective in the presentation. It is seldom effective for an advocate to sprawl head long after tripping over a loose cable.

4.33 Technological Exhibits and Visual Aids

In most cases, simple and inexpensive visual aids and demonstrative exhibits are appropriate and may be very effective. In other cases, the following technology may be useful:

Computer generated graphics.

Computer designed graphics can be made efficiently and economically with inexpensive software and color printers, without or with the need for artists and graphic designers.

Computer generated reconstructions and working models.

Reconstructions and models can be created by experts who can develop computer models and scale models. The advantage of the computer model is that the viewer can observe the exhibit from various angles and can be taken through the inside of an exhibit. The advantage of a scale model is that it can stay in view of the fact finder for a longer period of time. The cost of reconstructions and models varies widely.

Bar code readers.

Devices used by stores to read the prices on merchandise can be used by the advocate to present exhibits, review photographs, and retrieve any item placed in the computer. With an exhibit list the advocate can access anything in a computer for use during the trial or hearing. With the bar code reader the advocate can present on the screen all or parts of any evidence with the press of a button.

Illustrative marking pens.

Commentators and scientists use a device to diagram plays or explain experiments. Evidence presented through computer models, videos, or other exhibits can be illustrated and highlighted through the use of this marking device.

Visual presenters.

These devices project images from a document directly onto a television or large screen. Text, photographs, other exhibits, and the advocate's scribbled writing can be easily projected.

Computer exhibits.

In the court or hearing room, computers may be used to present duplicate copies of exhibits. For example, if a verdict form has been placed in the computer through an optical scanning device, the advocate can call up the form through the bar code reader or through the computer file retrieval system. The advocate can type in the answers on the form and highlight the important parts through the use of the illustrative marking pen.

Computer transcripts.

Some courtrooms are equipped with computers operated by court reporters that reproduce transcripts simultaneously while the witness testifies. These court rooms have equipment which provide the judge and advocates with immediate access to the transcript. With this system it is possible to highlight portions of a transcript, to ask questions for later research, and to print contemporaneous transcripts.

Virtual reality.

Fact finders can be fitted with optical-retina 3D electronic goggle-helmets which portray past events. The fact finders can decide based on their being an actual eye witness to the sights, sounds, and smells of an event. O.K., so it's an idea whose time has not yet come.

G. OBJECTIONS TO THE INTRODUCTION AND USE OF EXHIBITS

4.34 How to Prepare for Objections

The advocate must anticipate and prepare for any possible objections to the introduction of an exhibit which the opponent might raise. An objection, whether sustained or overruled, slows the presentation of the exhibit and the case.

4.35 How to Respond to Objections

If an objection to the introduction of an item of real evidence is sustained, the advocate has a number of options. An offer of proof may explain the exhibit and the grounds for its admissibility. The advocate may also avoid the evidentiary objection by offering the exhibit for a limited purpose. The exhibit may be offered as demonstrative evidence, and not as real evidence. The foundation for demonstrative evidence is less than that required for the introduction of real evidence and may permit the exhibit to be received for illustrative purposes. For example, in an assault case, if the advocate cannot prove the actual baseball bat used during the assault is the bat offered as real evidence, the bat could be offered as demonstrative evidence to assist the witness in testifying and to help the fact finder understand what happened.

4.36 Questioning By the Opponent

The opponent may question the witness after an exhibit has been offered to determine if there is a basis for an objection or to lay a foundation for an objection. The advocate may ask questions (also called voir dire) to determine whether the required foundation for the exhibit is lacking.

Sample Dialogue

Opponent:

Q: May I ask some questions of this witness for the purpose of laying a foundation for an objection to the introduction of this exhibit?

The scope of this voir dire examination is very limited. The questions should not be about the weight to be given the exhibit but only about the foundation. Voir dire examination should not be used unless the exhibit is likely to be excluded. Cross-examination is a more effective tool to reduce the evidentiary effect of an exhibit. The proponent of the exhibit has the right to object if the questioning goes beyond the scope of the intended purpose of that questioning.

4.37 Common Objections

Exhibits like other evidence are subject to any available and appropriate evidentiary objectives. Some common objections include:

> Irrelevant. Fed.R.Evid. 401–402.
>
> Unfairly prejudicial or gruesome. Fed.R.Evid. 403.
>
> Misleading or inaccurate. Fed.R.Evid. 403.
>
> Waste of time or undue delay. Fed.R.Evid. 403.
>
> Exhibit does not assist the witness or aid the fact finder. Fed.R.Evid. 401.
>
> Cumulative or repetitious. Fed.R.Evid. 403.
>
> Lack of foundation, authentication, and identification. Fed.R.Evid. 901–903.
>
> Inadmissible hearsay. Fed.R.Evid. 801–803.
>
> Violation of original writing rule. Fed.R.Evid. 1002.
>
> Constitutional objections in criminal actions (i.e., denial of right to cross-examine).

4.38 Unfairly Prejudicial Exhibits

Sample Dialogue

The prosecutor wishes to introduce a two foot by three foot color photograph displaying the victim's dead body found at the scene of the crime.

Prosecutor:

> The state offers State's Exhibit No. 3, a photograph of the victim's body, which shows there were two separate shotgun blasts: one to the head, and one to the knees.

Defense Counsel:

> Objection, your Honor. This exhibit is revolting, gruesome, and unfairly prejudicial. It has little probative value because the state's medical expert already testified to the cause of death. There is no reason for the jury to be shocked by the display of this photograph.

Prosecutor:

> May I be heard?

Judge:

> Yes.

Prosecutor:

> This photograph establishes there were two separate shots, supporting the state's claim of premeditation. It is essential for the jurors to see this photograph.

Judge:

> The objection will be sustained as to state's Exhibit No. 3. It is unnecessarily large and unfairly prejudicial.

Prosecutor:

> We have a smaller 8–inch by 10–inch color photograph of the same scene which we now offer as state's Exhibit No. 4.

Defense Counsel:

> We continue to object. There is no need for this photograph to be introduced and no need for it to be in color.

Judge:

> Objection overruled. State's Exhibit No. 4 is received.

Defense Counsel:

> We request that the photograph only be shown to the entire panel of jurors for several seconds and that it not be used by the state again during this trial.

Judge:

> I will allow each individual juror to briefly view the photograph and permit the state to refer to the photograph during summation, but not show it to the jury again.

Problems can be anticipated and resolved in advance. The offering advocate can:

PREPARE ALTERNATIVE pieces of demonstrative evidence if the initial exhibit is held not to be admissible. Some advocates will also have prepared a large black and white photograph as another alternative exhibit, if not allowed to introduce a color photograph into evidence.

EXPLAIN THE EXHIBIT provides the fact finder with relevant and realistic facts which are essential to an understanding of the case.

BRING A MOTION in limine to obtain a preliminary ruling as to its admissibility.

4.39 Emotionally Laden Exhibits

Sample Dialogue

The plaintiff lost both legs in an accident. The defendant provided plaintiff with prosthetic devices as artificial legs. The plaintiff sues the defendant for a defective prosthesis.

Examiner:

> We offer as demonstrative evidence Plaintiff's Exhibit No. 12, a videotape which shows the difficulty the plaintiff has in putting on and wearing the prosthesis and the defects in the product.

Opponent:

> Objection. This videotape is unfairly prejudicial as it plays to the passion and prejudice of the fact finder, which substantially outweighs its minimal probative value. Further, this evidence is repetitive because the plaintiff has already testified to the difficulty he has had with the prosthesis. However, we are willing to stipulate to the introduction of a still photograph of the plaintiff wearing the prosthesis.

Judge:

> Overruled. The plaintiff is entitled to show the jury how improperly the artificial limb fits.

In preparing the exhibit, the advocate may:

> PREPARE A REALISTIC videotape and not a staged effort that exaggerates what is displayed.

> INTRODUCE the demonstrative evidence before substantial evidence has been introduced which may trigger an objection on the grounds of repetition.

> HAVE THE WITNESS perform a reasonable live demonstration instead of the video demonstration.

4.40 Misleading or Time Consuming Exhibits

Demonstrative evidence may mislead or confuse the fact finder or distort the facts. Drawings which are not drawn to scale, photographs taken of the scene at a time far removed from the incident, models that are not substantially similar to the real evidence, and computer graphics which may present only part of the information or be deceptive in simplicity are examples of misleading situations.

Sample Dialogue

In a wrongful death action in which the plaintiff has died from injuries sustained in an automobile collision, the plaintiff's accident reconstruction expert witness has prepared a diagram of the scene.

Examiner:

> Plaintiff offers Plaintiff's Exhibit No. 10, a diagram of the scene prepared by our expert witness to reconstruct what happened on that day.

Opponent:

> Objection. This diagram is misleading and confusing and distorts the facts. The expert who prepared the diagram has no personal knowledge of the accident, this diagram is not drawn to precise scale, and this diagram does not include all of the evidence in this case to be introduced concerning the accident.

Examiner:

> In response to the objection, this diagram will help the fact finders understand the testimony by our expert witness and will help explain the facts in this case.

Judge:

> Overruled. Plaintiff's Exhibit No. 10 received.

Sometimes a presentation of demonstrative evidence may be time consuming or require extensive preparation. In these instances, the value of the demonstrative evidence must be weighed against the cost of court time and delay. Demonstrative evidence that does not significantly add to the case will frequently be rejected; for example, when the evidence will take a long time to be presented or when alternative ways of introducing the evidence, through oral testimony by witnesses, may be sufficient.

4.41 Unconstitutional Exhibits

In criminal cases, the introduction of demonstrative evidence may be objectionable as a violation of the defendant's constitutional right to cross-examine the witnesses. The defendant may not be able to cross-examine the person who created the exhibits. This objection is best used in conjunction with another ground supporting an objection.

Sample Dialogue

Prosecutor:

> Your Honor, I offer State's Exhibit N—the police report.

Defense Counsel:

> Objection, your Honor. This is not within the public record exception to hearsay. The report is conclusory, and my client has a right to cross-examine the officer who prepared this report.

Prosecutor:

> Your Honor, we wish to use the diagram on the lower third of the report as demonstrative evidence of the burglary scene and offer that portion of Exhibit N.

Judge:

> The diagram part of State's Exhibit N is admitted as illustrative evidence. The verbal remarks and conclusions surrounding the diagram must be masked and not visible on the exhibit.

Prosecutor:

> Your Honor, we have prepared an overhead transparency showing only the diagram.

Judge:

> You may proceed. The transparency will be marked as Exhibit N–1 and received into evidence.

4.42 Art Exhibits

If life as an advocate becomes too overwhelming, go to an art exhibit and renew your perspective on life.

RESOURCES

Bibliography

Access to Trial Exhibits in Civil Suits (case note), Kevin J. Mulry, 60 *St. John's L. R.* 358–371 (1986).

Demonstrative Trial Technique: The Introduction of Illustrative Exhibits, Jersey M. Green, 14 *Trial Diplomacy J.* 65–71 (1991).

How to Track Trial Exhibits Using Concordance, Patricia S. Eyres, 3 *L. Office Computing* 70 (1993).

Preparation and Use of State-of-the-Art Demonstrative Evidence, Terry L. Shapiro, 5 *National Trial Lawyer* 13 (1993).

Tangible Evidence: How to Use Exhibits at Trial (book reviews), Deanne C. Siemer, A, 22 *California Western L. R.* 203 (1985).

Trying Cases Visually, J. Rick Gass (Minnesota State Bar Association Continuing Legal Education 1992).

Using Demonstrative Evidence in Civil Trials, Mark A. Dombroff (Practicing Law Institute 1982).

Video Techniques in Trial and Pretrial, Fred I. Heller (Practicing Law Institute 1983).

Walkin' and Talkin' Exhibits into Evidence (Texas), David Schlueter, 56 *Texas Bar J.* 83 (1993).

Video

Demonstrative Evidence, National Institute For Trial Advocacy (1979).

Evidentiary Objections, National Institute For Trial Advocacy (1979).

Introduction of Exhibits, Trial Practice, Anderson Publishing (1990).

Introduction and Use of Exhibits, National Institute For Trial Advocacy (1979).

Laying the Foundation for Exhibits and Witnesses at Trial, National Institute For Trial Advocacy (1983).

Liturgy of Foundation, National Institute For Trial Advocacy (1979).

Problem Witness Tactics, National Institute For Trial Advocacy (1979).

Film

Who Framed Roger Rabbit? (1991).

Ghostbusters II (1989).

Star Wars (1978).

Easy Rider (1962).

The Ten Commandments (1957).

Citizen Kane (1948).

Gone with the Wind (1932).

INDEX